LOST RAILWAYS
OF
HAMPSHIRE

Leslie Oppitz

COUNTRYSIDE BOOKS

NEWBURY, BERKSHIRE

First published 2001
© Leslie Oppitz 2001
Reprinted 2003

COUNTRYSIDE BOOKS
3 Catherine Road
Newbury, Berkshire

To view our complete range of books,
please visit us at
www.countrysidebooks.co.uk

ISBN 1 85306 689 3

The cover picture shows N Class locomotive no 31874
hauling the first official passenger train of the Mid-Hants
Railway from Alton to Alresford on 25th May 1985.
(From an original painting by Colin Doggett
based on a photograph taken by Mike Esau)

Produced through MRM Associates Ltd., Reading
Typeset by Techniset Typesetters, Newton-le-Willows
Printed by Woolnough Bookbinding Ltd., Irthlingborough

CONTENTS

ABBREVIATIONS

The following abbreviations are used in this book:

A&R	Andover & Redbridge Railway
DN&SR	Didcot, Newbury & Southampton Railway
GWR	Great Western Railway
L&NWR	London & North Western Railway
L&SR	London & Southampton Railway
L&SWR	London & South Western Railway
LB&SCR	London, Brighton & South Coast Railway
LCGB	Locomotive Club of Great Britain
LMR	Longmoor Military Railway
M&SWJ	Midland & South Western Junction Railway
LRT	Light Rail Transit
RCTS	Railway Correspondence & Travel Society
S&DJR	Somerset & Dorset Junction Railway
S&DR	Southampton & Dorchester Railway
SCTS	Southern Counties Touring Society
SER	South Eastern Railway

Please note:
Junction implies a railway station
junction means where railway lines meet

ACKNOWLEDGEMENTS

Acknowledgements are due to the many libraries and record offices throughout Hampshire where staff have delved into records, and to the following for their help in supplying many early pictures: John H. Meredith, Mike Esau, Isle of Wight Railway Co, Rod K. Blencowe and Stations UK. Thanks also to Bill Trite, Chairman of the Swanage Railway Company Ltd, for his help given by identifying many early locomotives and to Colin Doggett for his splendid cover picture.

Thanks also go to the following who assisted: The Isle of Wight Steam Railway, Mid-Hants Railway, Alex Evans of East Tisted station, Paul Lidgeley of Old Burghclere, Lloyd Lay, Director, White Horse Ferries (Hythe Pier Railway) and John Bosworth, Curator of Bishop's Waltham Museum.

Finally, thanks go to Kevin Robertson for his research when preparing the book *Hampshire Railways Remembered*, published in 1988, which was written jointly with the author of this book. Also thanks as ever to my wife, Joan, for her patience and assistance.

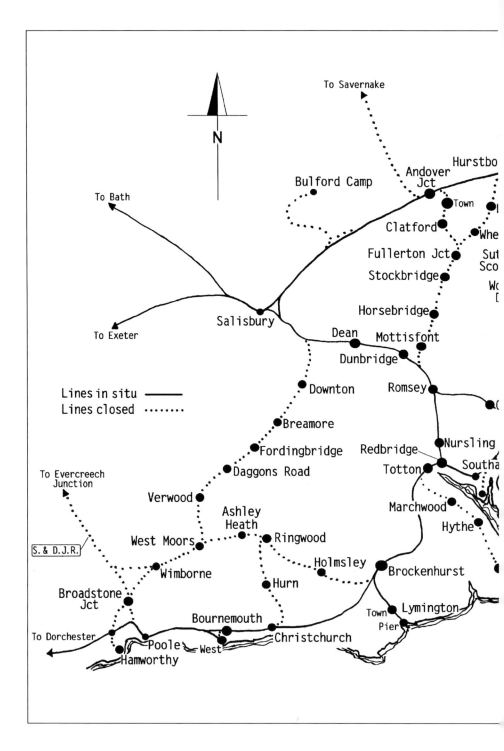

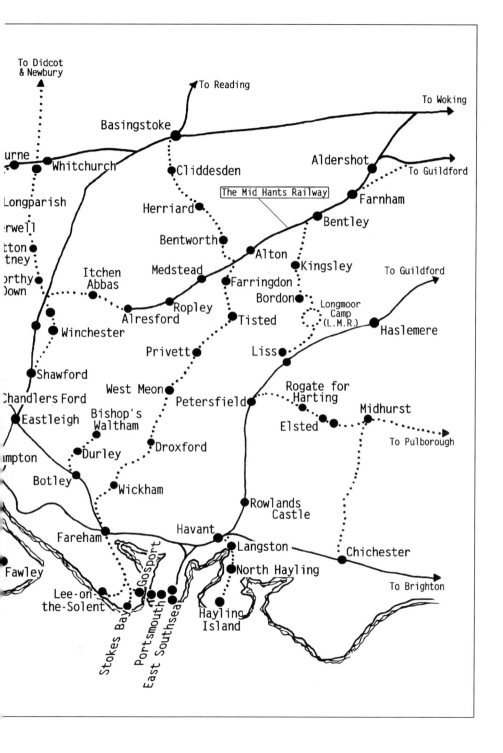

Introduction

A steam train hauled by Ivatt tank locomotive 2MT no 41312 pulls into Alresford station. Soon the platform is crowded as many passengers alight, some with excited children pulling parents along behind them. This scene could have taken place during any summer month in the early 1900s when the railways enjoyed great popularity. Yet it was a May Bank Holiday in the year 2000 and a Mid-Hants Railway train had just pulled in from Ropley on the restored Watercress Line, formerly part of the London & South Western Railway (L&SWR) route between Winchester and Alton.

The above scene typified earlier times throughout many parts of Hampshire. Today many branch lines in the county have disappeared. Former station buildings, signal boxes, road bridges or overgrown trackbeds all go to make up what was once a vast network of railways when steam trains made their way across open stretches of countryside, linking remote villages and towns.

First ideas for a railway in Hampshire came when a line was proposed linking London with Southampton in 1831 but it was not until July 1834 that the necessary Act of Parliament was obtained allowing construction to begin. At that time Southampton was little more than a fishing village, although it was fast showing signs of development into a commercial port. Therefore, in the opinion of the promoters, Southampton was more worthy of a railway than naval Portsmouth. The London & Southampton line was opened throughout on 11th May 1840. The final section between Basingstoke and Winchester crossed chalk uplands through deep cuttings and passed through several tunnels.

Even before the main line was completed, several railway promoters were looking towards Portsmouth and its naval traffic, but they had not reckoned with opposition from the naval authorities. So instead, in 1841, a branch from Bishopstoke (later called Eastleigh) to Gosport was opened, with the intention of tapping the Portsmouth traffic via a ferry service across the harbour. This was the first branch line in the county.

During the 1840s, a period which became known as 'Railway Mania', many new proposals were put forward. As far as Hampshire was concerned the main intentions were twofold. These were to extend westwards towards Exeter and also to provide a north-south link which did not involve the transhipment of goods via London. These were further indications of how Southampton was developing as a commercial port.

Part of this plan was realised in 1847 with the opening of an extension westwards from Bishopstoke to Salisbury and, in the same year, the Southampton to Dorchester line was built with the intention of reaching Exeter via a coastal route. In December 1848 a north-south link was achieved with the opening of the Reading to Basingstoke branch. Although this provided the connection required, there was a problem. The line was built to Brunel's GWR broad gauge of 7' 0¼" while the remainder of the railways in Hampshire were built to the standard or narrow gauge of 4' 8½". The Great Western Railway (GWR), with its Basingstoke branch, now had a foothold in Hamphire.

Elsewhere in the county, the same period saw the monopoly of the L&SWR broken when a London, Brighton & South Coast Railway (LB&SCR) line from Shoreham and Chichester reached Portsmouth. This plus the GWR line sowed the seeds of conflict between the rival companies for many years to come.

By the end of the 1840s the railway bubble in Hampshire had burst and during the years 1848 to 1852 only one new line was built, from Fareham to Cosham. The final stages in the development of the main routes came during the period 1852 to 1854 with the extension of the L&SWR lines from Farnham to Alton, and from Basingstoke to Andover and eventually Salisury.

Further routes followed. A direct line to Portsmouth was one of the first priorities, although hostility between the L&SWR and the LB&SCR came near to open warfare as gangs of workers confronted each other armed with spades, picks and shovels. Less dramatically, the broad gauge Reading to Basingstoke line had been provided with a third set of rails laid to the narrow gauge, so it could be used by non-GWR trains.

The L&SWR's idea of an alternative north-south connection, bypassing the GWR, was far from dead. The GWR had its sights throughout on the South Coast ports, but it was not prepared to openly promote a new line itself. This was because the company was going through a difficult period, conflict elsewhere having drained its resources. Were it not for this temporary shortage of funds, broad gauge trains might well have succeeded in reaching Southampton.

As it was, the strength of the GWR was thrown behind schemes like the Andover & Redbridge Railway (A&R). This was a nominally independent concern promoting a north–south line to connect with the L&SWR just west of Southampton. Here at least a famous victory was won by the L&SWR. Unknown to the GWR, the Andover & Redbridge promoters had been playing one giant company off against the other. The L&SWR came off best, and the spectre of the GWR's broad gauge retreated from what was considered by the shareholders to be unassailable L&SWR territory.

The GWR was certainly not beaten. It was most active behind the Didcot, Newbury & Southampton Railway, but due to shortage of hard cash, the GWR reached only as far south as Winchester (Chesil) to then join the L&SWR line north of Shawford. Had this not been the case Southampton would certainly have been served by a rival route to both London and the Midlands and much of the ensuing railway history of the county could have been very different indeed.

In addition to these grand projects a number of minor lines and branches sprang up, some promoted by small groups or individuals primarily to serve local needs. Of these the Bishop's Waltham, Stokes Bay, Southsea and Netley lines were typical examples.

The final decades of the 19th century were a time of consolidation. Cut-off routes and blocking lines were opened by the L&SWR to either shorten an existing route or attempt yet again to thwart the advances of the GWR. When a line opened in 1888 between Brockenhurst and Christchurch, improved services to Bournemouth became possible, avoiding a circuitous route via

12

Ringwood. Such was the new route's popularity that a Pullman car was placed in service in 1890.

Elsewhere a line from Hurstbourne to Fullerton was built with the intention of stopping the southward progress of the GWR-backed Didcot, Newbury & Southampton Railway. From 1903 onwards the Meon Valley line from Alton to Fareham made possible a more direct route between London and Gosport, while at the same time countering GWR efforts to reach Portsmouth. But any advantages this new route offered were certainly not acted upon by the L&SWR and the Meon Valley line may be suitably referred to as one of the less successful of Hampshire's railways.

The last new line to be built in Hampshire connected Totton with Fawley and was opened as recently as 1925. Passenger traffic was small from the start, but the promoters recognised that the main potential was freight, principally from the oil refinery which dwarfed the little terminus.

This book intends to examine not only the lives of these 'lost' lines, their decline and closure but also visits a preserved railway of today, the Mid-Hants Railway, dedicated to keeping the past alive. The book provides the reader with a means to explore the many stations and trackbeds that have survived.

Leslie Oppitz

1
Trains Along The Test Valley

Romsey/Fullerton Junction/Andover
Hurstbourne to Fullerton Junction

A special excursion organised by the SCTS at Fullerton on 2nd September 1962 hauled by ex-L&SWR Drummond 700 class 0-6-0 locomotive no 30309. The line from Andover to Romsey closed to passenger traffic in 1964. (John H. Meredith)

Romsey/Fullerton Junction/Andover

On 12th July 1858 Royal Assent was granted to the Andover & Redbridge Railway Company (A&R) for a line to be built by converting a canal (opened 1792) along much of the route as well as running parallel to the rivers Test and Avon. Just over a year later on 28th September 1859 there were great celebrations for the townsfolk of Romsey. As a 14-gun salute was fired in a field near Broadlands at Romsey, Lord Palmerston, then resident at Broadlands House, cut the first sod of the new line. The branch would join the Salisbury to Southampton line at Kimbridge, just north of Romsey. Despite the branch's fine opening ceremony, little other work was done and the independent concern was declared bankrupt in 1861. A battle followed between the L&SWR and the GWR to gain control over the unfinished project although this was settled the following year with the L&SWR taking over the entire route.

The Andover to Romsey section finally opened to passenger traffic on 6th March 1865. The line had numerous sharp curves, a direct consequence of following a canal and two rivers. This was

A deserted and forgotten Clatford station (January 1969) on the Andover-Fullerton branch. The station opened in March 1865 and lasted almost 100 years. (R.K.Blencowe)

15

A steam train arrives at Fullerton Junction station c1910. Originally called Fullerton Bridge station, it became Fullerton Junction following the opening of the connection with Hurstbourne in 1885. (R.K.Blencowe)

Fullerton Junction looking towards Stockbridge, photographed in January 1969, five years after closure of the line. (R.K.Blencowe)

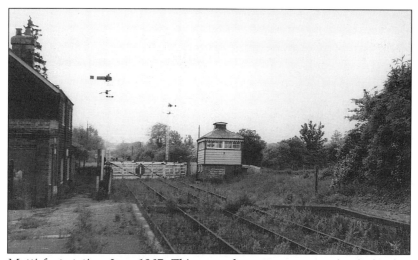

Mottisfont station, June 1967. This was a busy passenger station in its time and also catered for goods trains transporting chalk and lime from a local quarry. (R.K.Blencowe)

Looking southwards at the former Horsebridge station on the Andover to Romsey line. Photographed June 1967. (R.K.Blencowe)

17

a handicap to fast running, so during the early 1880s considerable straightening of the line was carried out. Also in 1865 a Midland & South Western Junction (M&SWJ) line reached Andover from the north, thus a through north-south route became available.

In 1885 Fullerton Bridge station was renamed Fullerton Junction following the opening of a short branch from Hurstbourne. The development of the A&R was now complete. Meanwhile the line had acquired the nickname 'Sprat & Winkle' – although from where is not clear.

Along the route stations were very much focal points for the communities they served, although in accordance with railway tradition they were not always ideally situated. Mottisfont was, for example, some way from the village of the same name, while Horsebridge took its name from the nearby mill and not the larger King's Somborne village one mile or so distant.

The exception to this was Stockbridge, located in the centre of

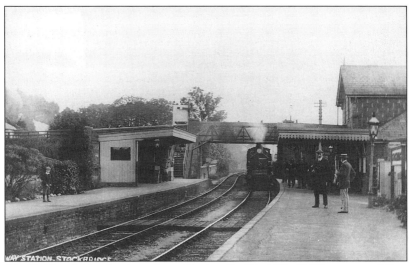

Stockbridge station in steam days. During the First World War many soldiers were stationed in the surrounding area and the station was used frequently for troop movements. (R.K.Blencowe)

18

what still is a delightful mid-Hampshire town with a wide High Street and many bow-fronted shops on either side. The station was built in a style in keeping with the town, with small narrow windows curved at the top. Stockbridge was also the busiest station between Andover and Romsey. It drew considerable trade from commuters and scholars and there was also a reasonable-sized goods yard, serviced by a pick-up goods train which ran once daily in each direction. The engine would spend some time at Stockbridge shunting the wagons into their required positions, and a small water tower was provided for its benefit. A racecourse also existed at Stockbridge for some years prior to 1900 and the transport of horses from the several nearby racing stables was a valuable source of revenue to the railway almost up to the time of closure.

At the northern end of the line Andover Town station, as it

Fullerton station building, today a private residence. The awning was acquired from Brighton station in Sussex. It is said that Fullerton station was upgraded during its existence to honour Queen Victoria who twice visited the station. (Author)

Horsebridge station, May 2000. Although private property the platforms and station building have been preserved. (Author)

was known, stood ideally situated for the main shopping centre, although in later years the competition was uncomfortably close to hand in the form of an adjacent bus station. The Town station was also far more convenient than the Junction station on the busy Basingstoke to Salisbury line. The Town station's disadvantage was a level crossing immediately at the end of the platform, the cause of numerous long delays to road users.

Andover was also the home of the now famous Tasker Engineering Company. Traction engines, steam rollers and trailers produced by the Andover factory are still seen at rallies throughout the country. The company had the use of a private siding which branched off the line just south of Andover Town station.

The line throughout from Andover to Romsey was one of the first to be operated by diesel units in 1957. It soon became apparent that there was insufficient revenue to be accrued from what had become a rural line. The former M&SWJ route closed

The signal box at Horsebridge station has been acquired from Yalding in Kent. The station closed to regular passenger traffic in September 1964. (Author)

An early L&SWR coach at Horsebridge was acquired from BR at Bournemouth, today making useful additional accommodation. (Author)

in 1961 and with it went the through traffic which was formerly routed down the A&R. Consequently the Andover to Romsey section became one of the first diesel casualties in Hampshire, the last passenger train running in September 1964. A period of dereliction followed along the line with final demolition coming a few years later. By the autumn of 1969, much of the railway north of Romsey had vanished.

Yet numerous reminders still exist. At Fullerton the original station building is privately owned and an awning (acquired from Brighton station in Sussex) over the former platform recalls earlier times. According to previous owners the waiting room fireplace inside the property was upgraded during its existence to honour Queen Victoria who, it has been claimed, twice used Fullerton station to visit Benjamin Disraeli who occupied nearby Tescombe House.

Mottisfont station building, enlarged since closure in 1964, photographed in May 2000. In the early 1920s seven trains each way stopped at the station on weekdays providing a service between Romsey and Southampton. (Author)

Further south, the original railway atmosphere has been recaptured at Horsebridge station where the platforms have been restored to their former glory. Again it is private property, but the owners have done much to recall the past. An early L&SWR coach acquired from the former BR at Bournemouth stands in the station and a signal box rescued from Yalding in Kent replaces the original.

Mottisfont station bustled with activity in its heyday, not only serving the surrounding village but in addition goods trains transporting chalk and lime from the local quarry, much of it exported to Canada. After closure in 1964, the station building became dilapidated but today it has become 'The Old Station' – another attractive private property.

Hurstbourne to Fullerton Junction

In 1882 the L&SWR obtained powers to build a short double-track branch line from Hurstbourne on the main Basingstoke to Salisbury line, to Fullerton on the existing Andover to Romsey branch. The branch opened on 1st June 1885 with traffic at a very low level.

The story of intrigue and double-dealing behind the scenes concerning this branch had its origins in 1873 when an independent line was promoted from Didcot, through Newbury to a junction on the main Southampton line just north of Micheldever. Understandably the L&SWR was considerably against the intrusion whereas the GWR was very much in favour, recognising that the proposal offered the possibility of a foothold in its rival's territory.

The GWR had its eyes on the port of Southampton. Although unwilling to openly support the new line for fear of causing difficulties between itself and the L&SWR elsewhere, it was certainly active behind the scenes. The plan for the line was changed, to become a completely independent route from Newbury to Southampton, running through Whitchurch and Winchester. At no point would the trains run on L&SWR rails.

Wherwell station and goods yard, c1910. Agricultural products were a main source of freight revenue. Hay loaded in the truck in the foreground required sheeting as protection against sparks from the engine. (R.K.Blencowe)

The L&SWR, seeing its monopoly threatened, offered access to Southampton via Romsey with the new line from Hurstbourne to Fullerton under its control. The suggested route was therefore Newbury-Whitchurch-Hurstbourne-Fullerton-Romsey-Southampton. Indeed it hoped that by going ahead with the Hurstbourne line the temptation to link up would be too strong for the independent concern to resist and the L&SWR would thus benefit from the Newbury traffic. In reality this nearly came about, for the Didcot, Newbury & Southampton was suffering a severe cash shortage. The L&SWR was well aware of this.

Armed with this knowledge, the L&SWR went ahead with construction of the Hurstbourne-Fullerton line. The GWR-backed Didcot, Newbury & Southampton was meantime pressing further south in an attempt to reach the coast. In the event, it got as far as Winchester, then stopped. There was little likelihood of the line extending any further, but the GWR was much too far south to be interested in a link-up with the L&SWR

at Hurstbourne. The result was a stalemate, and the L&SWR found itself with a 7½ mile line serving no real need.

Nevertheless, on lst July 1885, a service of three passenger trains each way daily commenced on the new line, which for reasons now forgotten was dubbed the 'Nile Valley Railway'. The trains ran between Whitchurch and Fullerton with two intermediate stations on the branch. These were Longparish and Wherwell. Each had lavish accommodation for passengers and goods which was far in excess of local requirements, having been designed to suit the Newbury to Southampton trade.

The service was later increased to five trains each way on weekdays only, but the line was still poorly patronised. The locals found little use for the facilities the stations offered:

The handling of Goods, Passengers, Parcels, Furniture, Vans, Carriages, Portable Engines, Machines on Wheels, Livestock, Horse Boxes and Prize Cattle Vans.

The Hurstbourne-Fullerton line attracted few passengers and economies were soon effected. This steam railmotor, seen here at Longparish, was photographed c1905. (R.K.Blencowe)

Wherwell station building is today used as private residences, still carrying the date 1884. The L&SWR had hoped the Hurstbourne-Fullerton route would reach main-line status but during its life it only acquired use in a diversionary capacity. (Author)

There was one way in which the short branch did fulfil a useful role, and that was as a diversionary route to Southampton and Eastleigh. Considering the poor receipts, operating costs were high and in an effort to reduce these a steam railmotor, the forerunner of today's railcars, was tried. It failed to increase patronage sufficiently so in 1913 the route was reduced to a single track throughout. The ensuing years saw a further decline in what was a meagre revenue and it came as no surprise when it was announced that passenger services would be withdrawn from 6th July 1931. The section from Hurstbourne to Longparish was to be totally abandoned.

There was a brief boom in freight traffic during the Second World War, when Harewood Forest took on a new role as an ammunition dump. Extra sidings and trains were provided but it

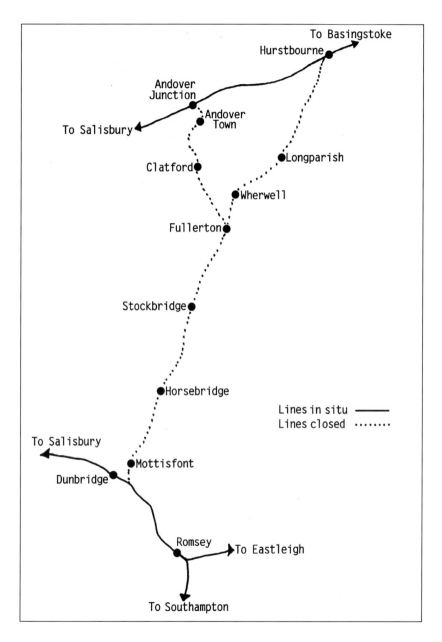

was a temporary reprieve. The short branch closed in 1956, after which the rails were torn up.

Today, more than a century after closure, traces of the former line can still be found. At Wherwell the road still crosses the railway bridge and the nearby station house carries the date 1884. Whilst visiting Wherwell in May 2000 the author called at the White Lion public house to ask the way. On leaving a local called out, 'You've missed the last train!'

2
A GWR Line To Newbury

Winchester/Newbury

A passenger train hauled by 0-6-0 ex-GWR Collett class 22XX steams alongside the 'Winchester Bypass', c1953. (R.K.Blencowe)

It is just over 40 years since a regular passenger train service operated between Winchester and Newbury. The handful of passengers who were among the line's last few customers have long since found alternative means of covering the 27 miles between the two towns. Yet the closure of this railway represented more than the demise of just another branch line. It was the last vestige of GWR influence in Hampshire, although during the dark days of the Second World War it proved a lifeline between the Midlands and South Coast ports.

The route itself dates back to 1885 when the independent

Ex-L&SWR Drummond class T9 4-4-0 no 30287 heading a passenger train arrives at Winchester Chesil station from Newbury in the 1950s. The Didcot, Newbury & Southampton Railway (DN&SR) operated by the GWR had attempted to reach Southampton but funds had run out. Eventually a compromise was reached allowing DN&SR trains to use L&SWR lines. (R.K.Blencowe)

Didcot, Newbury & Southampton Railway Company (DN&SR) had driven its line southwards as far as Winchester in the hope of reaching Southampton. But funds ran out and, after six years of failing to raise the additional capital required, the DN&SR was forced into a compromise situation. In 1891, in return for the L&SWR providing a connection into its own Southampton line just south of Winchester, the DN&SR was compelled to renounce all intention of pursuing an independent route.

Thus, for almost 75 years, trains ran across the Berkshire and Hampshire Downs to Winchester. The line was operated by the GWR, but locomotives had to be changed before the final few miles to Southampton owing to the rivalry between the L&SWR and the GWR. Whenever a train from Newbury reached Winchester the GWR engine had to be uncoupled and driven

Trains from Winchester Chesil joined the L&SWR line at Shawford junction, south of Winchester. Ex-GWR locomotive no 3440 'City of Truro' with passenger set travels southwards bound for Eastleigh, probably early 1950s. This is reputed to be the first engine to have reached 100 mph earlier in the century. (R.K.Blencowe)

clear to make way for a waiting L&SWR engine, which was then reversed into position and coupled up. The passengers remained in their carriages while this time-consuming manoeuvre took place. A similar performance occurred when trains arrived from Southampton. Not surprisingly most passengers for South-ampton from Didcot and the North travelled via Reading and Basingstoke, the service being quicker and more efficient.

Winchester Chesil station, as it became known, was therefore an oasis of the GWR in what was recognised L&SWR territory. Surprisingly the staff at Chesil outnumbered those at the main-line station quite considerably. As well as the stationmaster, there was an army of clerks, foremen, porters, shunters, warehousemen, carters, guards, drivers, firemen and cleaners. Some of these were only required because of the engine changing manoeuvres. In addition there was the station cat, an

31

*An ex-GWR Collett 0-6-0 class 22XX hauling a passenger set approaches
Winchester Chesil station, c1950. In the background is St Catherine's Hill.
(S.C.Townroe/R.K.Blencowe)*

independent feline who, it was said, sported the correct livery
of the company.

The journey northwards from Winchester Chesil to Newbury
began with a tunnel under St Giles's Hill. The excavation had
proved contentious from an early date to the track gangs for, if
they were to qualify for extra pay in the form of tunnel
allowance, the tunnel concerned had to measure over 440 yards
in length. The Winchester tunnel measured only 439 yards. It
was, however, built on a curve and, upon appeal, the men
managed to get the longer side measured – which came out at
441 yards, just enough to earn them the extra allowance!

Between Winchester and Newbury there were eight intermediate stations. These were King's Worthy, Worthy Down,
Sutton Scotney, Whitchurch, Litchfield, Burghclere, Highclere
and Woodhay. All served rural communities and in themselves
they were hardly able to support the running costs of the route.
King's Worthy, the first station northwards from Winchester,

Highclere station, c1910. During the First World War the station was kept busy handling injured soldiers from the Western Front who were taken to Highclere Castle which became a temporary hospital. (Lens of Sutton)

was from about 1930 onwards the home base for a railway lorry service which operated around the Winchester area. Customers were able to benefit from a door-to-door service whereby goods and parcels of almost any description were collected by the railway lorry and then taken to the local station for despatch by train.

The next station was Worthy Down, opened in 1917 to serve the nearby Royal Flying Corps air station. Later the base became a naval air station and, during the Second World War, it was known as HMS *Kestrel*. A propaganda broadcast from Germany proudly proclaimed one night '. . . we have sunk HMS *Kestrel*'! Sutton Scotney station (today better known for its A34 Services Area) had the distinction of a climbing rose trained to form the letters GWR over the side of the goods shed.

Further north was the site of the short-lived halt at Barton Stacey, provided for the use of navvies occupied in building the nearby army camp of the same name in about 1941. The halt came to a sudden end, courtesy of these same navvies. After getting drunk one Christmas, they had a race between two traction engines which were driven towards the railway. Unfortunately the men were unable to stop their charges which ploughed relentlessly on over a field and eventually over the wooden platform of Barton Stacey halt, before coming to rest against the side of the railway cutting.

Nearby was the site of a wartime signal box at Lodge Bridge, provided to break the long section of single line between Sutton Scotney and Whitchurch and so allow more trains to be handled. Lodge Bridge must have been a desolate spot to work, as the man stationed there was unlikely to see another soul during his long shift, his only company often the incessant blowing of the wind. It gained the nickname 'Howls Lodge'.

The mid-point between Winchester and Newbury was Whitchurch, a station serving a fair-sized community complete with some industries. There was Portals, the banknote manu-

Looking southwards at Winchester Chesil (known as Winchester Cheesehill until 1949) in June 1965. The station closed to passenger traffic in March 1960 but survived until April 1966 for goods traffic. (R.K.Blencowe)

facturers, at nearby Overton, as well as the famous Whitchurch silk mill and a jam factory operated by J. Long. In the early years of the century the station boasted a one-legged porter, a poor unfortunate who came by his disability whilst in the forces and on whom the railway had taken pity. It is said he would hobble up to a passenger offering to carry the bags, knowing that the sight of his single leg would lead to polite refusal and, more often than not, a sympathetic tip for his willingness.

Northwards from Whitchurch the route climbed almost continuously and passed through a 60-foot deep chalk cutting at Larksborough. This excavation was a problem to the railway from the start owing to repeated chalk falls from the sheer cutting sides, which were sometimes enough to bury the rails beneath. Matters came to a head not long after the railway opened in 1885, when a large boulder of chalk dislodged itself from the cutting as a train was passing through and fell through the roof of a carriage, fortunately not causing any injuries. Following this, teams of workers were set to removing tons of the material which were carted away. Even so, the problems with falling chalk were to continue throughout the life of the line and, in the winter of 1947/8, hundreds of tons were removed and later sold to a talcum powder manufacturer. The general instability was traced to horizontal lines of flint running through the rock which would crack as a result of frost penetration and so bring down large quantities of chalk.

From Whitchurch, the next station was Litchfield, serving the tiny hamlet of the same name. Inevitably receipts from this station were always small and, in the quest for economy, the crossing loop and signal box were removed in the 1930s only to be reinstated a few years later when extra traffic was handled from 1942 onwards.

The line then reached its summit, passing under the shadow of Beacon Hill where the remains of an Iron Age hillfort stand 858 feet above sea level. Following this there was a gentle descent to Burghclere. From 1940 onwards this station was in the charge of a delightful lady, Bessie Shearman, who started work when many of the men were away serving with the forces, and who stayed on until the line closed.

Winchester Chesil station has today become a multi-storey car park but the tunnel entrance at the north end survives although blocked off. (Author)

From 1888 to about 1930 Burghclere benefited from a thriving lime industry. Chalk hewn from the nearby hills was burnt in kilns between alternate layers of coal to produce lime suitable for the building industry, while substandard or surplus material was sold to farmers as fertiliser. Almost all the coal and lime was moved by rail, a siding leading down to the quarry immediately south of the station. Unfortunately imports of cheap, inferior-quality lime spelled the end of production at Burghclere and the remains of the kilns and workings are now a nature reserve.

The next station was Highclere, which took its name from nearby Highclere Castle, the home of the Earl of Carnarvon who was one of the railway's early supporters. For this reason the station name did not exactly coincide with the location of the village. Highclere station was in the village of Burghclere, Burghclere station was in Old Burghclere village and Highclere village proper was served by Woodhay station. It is confusing enough now and it was no less confusing when the railway was operating and must have enraged many travellers over the years.

Burghclere station is located in Old Burghclere. The station building and platform have survived the years to become a private residence. (Author)

Highclere station handled mainly agricultural produce, but during the First World War it experienced a brisk traffic in injured soldiers. Several trainloads of men from the Western Front were taken to nearby Highclere Castle which, in keeping with other large houses elsewhere in the country, was converted into a temporary hospital. The last station before Newbury was Woodhay, which had, it was said, one platform in Hampshire and the other in Berkshire. Here the porter kept a pet goat tethered to the embankment, which was presumably kept very neatly grazed.

The DN&SR railway lost its independent status in 1923, passing totally into the hands of the GWR. This was accompanied by a slow decline in profits and, to counter this, the railway company removed the stationmasters from their posts and lifted little-used sections of track in an effort to reduce running costs.

With the advent of the Second World War the importance of the line as a through route to the South Coast was recognised, for

*King's Worthy station on the GWR route between Winchester and Newbury.
During the 1930s the station was established as a lorry base operating around
the Winchester area. (R.K.Blencowe)*

it was essential to have more than one north-south railway
available for the movement of men and equipment. This was
especially so during the period prior to the invasion of Europe.
The railway was closed throughout its length from August 1942
for some eight months while thousands of men were brought in
to re-equip the line for its future role.

Gone was the sleepy branch line. Improved crossing places
and new signal boxes sprang up almost overnight. Facilities
previously abandoned were reinstated, while south of Worthy
Down a new connection was cut through the chalk to link into
the main London-Southampton route. This was an insurance
measure, lest enemy action render a viaduct at Shawford
impassable. Fortunately such fears were never justified and for
months the trains poured southwards in an almost unbroken
stream. The traffic was so heavy that it was sometimes difficult
to later fit a reinstated passenger service into the timetable.

Once the Allies had gained a secure foothold in France,
however, the importance of the DN&SR began to wane, so that

38

Burghclere station. From 1888 to about 1930 the area benefited from a thriving lime industry. After closure the kilns and workings became a nature reserve. (Lens of Sutton)

A passenger train at Sutton Scotney hauled by GWR 2-4-0 locomotive designed by Dean and usually called 'Barnum' class. Picture probably mid-1920s. (R.K.Blencowe)

Winchester Chesil goods yard 1950, looking towards Chesil station. After final closure the area became part of an industrial estate. (S.C.Townroe/ R.K.Blencowe)

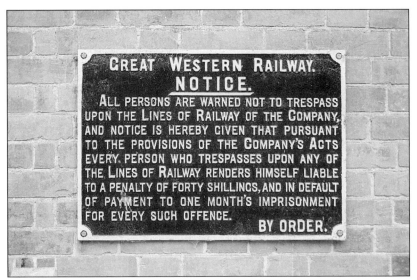

Dire consequences threaten trespassers as shown in this GWR notice fixed to the wall of the present Burghclere station building! (Author)

Highclere station building, south of Newbury, photographed May 2000. Today a private residence, the building has seen many alterations since its closure to passenger traffic in March 1960. (Author)

by the time of nationalisation and the advent of British Railways it had changed from an essential to an expensive part of the network. Economies soon began, starting with the closure of signal boxes and crossing loops. In addition the line suffered cancellation of some of its daytime services. There was also serious competition from the adjacent A34 trunk road to the Midlands. An ever-increasing flow of goods could be seen borne on the backs of lorries which trundled slowly up and briskly down the numerous humps characteristic of the old road to Newbury.

In March 1960 the line closed to passenger traffic with freight ending just six years later. With almost indecent haste, tracks were ripped up and bulldozers moved in to transform the trackbed into an improved A34. Decades later the motor lorries rumble where trains once ran and the old stations have vanished under new development. Winchester Chesil has become a multi-storey car park and the adjacent goods yard at Bar End is now an

41

industrial estate. The old station house still exists, reached by footpaths up St Giles's Hill. It is bricked and boarded up but, when visited by the author in May 2000, there were hopes it might be converted to a private residence. Elsewhere along the route the main A34 has taken over, lorries and cars travelling over what used to be the platforms at King's Worthy station.

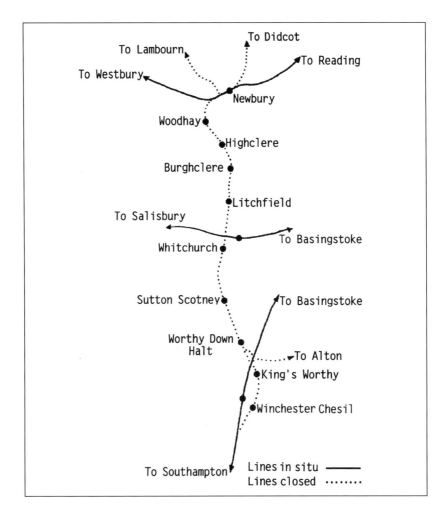

North of Whitchurch the railway has also disappeared under a highway and Larksborough cutting seems an insignificant feature next to the wide road. Stations converted to attractive private residences include Highclere, Burghclere and Whitchurch.

Yet the old railway is far from forgotten. Efforts have been made to trace memorabilia relating to the former GWR Didcot-Newbury-Winchester line. An exhibition at the Basingstoke Leisure Park, 'Milestones – Hampshire's Living History Museum', has been modelled on part of the former Winchester Chesil Street station and already includes two GWR noticeboards, a ticket barrier from Newbury and blue-black paving from Highclere station.

There is yet another reminder of the former line. On certain days at around 8.15 in the evening in a house built on the trackbed near Winchester, the house shakes. The time coincides almost exactly with that of the last train from Newbury to Winchester!

3
L&SWR Tracks Into Dorset

Salisbury/Fordingbridge/West Moors
Southampton/Brockenhurst/Ringwood/
Broadstone
Ringwood/Hurn/Christchurch

Fordingbridge station in earlier times. Unfortunately for local residents the station was situated some way out of the town. (R.K.Blencowe)

Salisbury/Fordingbridge/West Moors

Despite its authorisation on 22nd July 1861, the Salisbury & Dorset Junction Railway took over five years to build. The line, which passed through Hampshire, intended to bring about a 'much-needed improvement between Salisbury and the Dorset

*Today there is virtually no sign of Fordingbridge station (seen here late 1950s)
where the site became an industrial area. Only the name Station Road has
survived the years. (R.K.Blencowe)*

coast'. It left the Salisbury to Bishopstoke (later Eastleigh) branch
at Alderbury junction to join the Southampton & Dorchester
'Corkscrew' branch at West Moors. The route had originally
been planned to reach the coast with Poole included in the title
but the Act covered only the line to West Moors.

The line opened on 20th December 1866 and there were five
intermediate stations. These were at Downton, Breamore,
Fordingbridge, Daggons Road (initially named Alderholt) and
Verwood, all with single track but with passing loops at each.
West Moors, at the junction with the Southampton & Dorchester
Railway, was added on 1st August 1867. There were also no less
than six level crossings, while north of Fordingbridge there was a
private siding serving a Government store. Each station had
facilities for handling goods as well as passengers with
Fordingbridge by far the largest, having four sidings as well as
separate cattle pens and a goods warehouse. Initially the
independent line was worked by the L&SWR but in August

In the early 1920s some six trains each way called at Breamore on weekdays travelling between Bournemouth West and Salisbury, most with London (Waterloo) connections. (R.K.Blencowe)

1883 the L&SWR took it over completely.

On 3rd June 1884 there was a disastrous accident when the 4.33 pm service from Salisbury was derailed between Downton and Breamore, killing five passengers and injuring another 41. The train was reported to have been travelling at nearly 70 mph, well in excess of the speed allowed. The incident drew immediate attention to the poor state of the rolling stock and also the inadequate ballast along the track. This was a situation that had become typical of many backwater and non-profit-making branch lines. In its report, the Railway Inspectorate of the Board of Trade was highly critical over such failures. At Downton, the condition of the track had even been noticed by an outsider, the daughter of the local Rector, who found places where a number of keys had fallen out of the track's chairs so the rails were no longer adequately secured.

During its life the line settled for a quiet existence. Yet it proved useful to some extent as a diversion for north-south

Breamore station still survives almost 40 years after its complete closure. (Author)

trains, especially when the neighbouring Somerset & Dorset Junction Railway (S&DJR) line was overburdened. Several peak Saturday services used the route, especially during the 1950s, although the journey usually took longer. Another notable through service that survived a number of years was the overnight newspaper train from Waterloo to Weymouth via Salisbury.

In March 1963, the 'Beeching Plan' was published. Notice of closure of the Salisbury-West Moors line was announced very soon afterwards, at the end of June 1963. It was one of the first in the country to follow the plan's publication. Rising operating costs and wages had taken their toll and it was clear that stopping trains of three carriages with no more than 20 passengers could hardly pay their way. In fact closure had already been under consideration when the plan was published.

On 3rd March 1964 the Minister of Transport announced his consent to the closure subject to the provision of extra buses. This was to be effective from Monday, 4th May with the last trains

47

running on the previous Saturday. According to the *Salisbury Journal,* it was a night to remember when the last train left Salisbury bound for Bournemouth at 8.30 pm. A wreath bearing the legend 'Last passenger train to Bournemouth' was ceremoniously placed on the front of the locomotive, the reigning Fordingbridge Carnival Queen, Miss Valerie Knibbs, kissed the engine-driver and Salisbury's stationmaster, Mr S.J. Cooney, blew the final whistle. On board the streamer-bedecked train there were hundreds of people anxious to claim the memory of the last ride.

Passengers included more than 70 members of the Fordingbridge Camera Club, armed to the teeth with equipment, who were determined to commit the occasion to film. Along the line, crowds waved their personal farewells and 'Down with Beeching' posters were to be seen. Fordingbridge station was floodlit for photographers but such were the crowds that taking pictures proved difficult. A reporter quoted an elderly man, sandwiched between a teenager and a stout lady trying to

When visited by the author in September 2000, Breamore's 'Station House' was occupied by 87-year-old 'Dinky' Trim, the wife of the late Leslie Trim who had been in charge of the station. (Author)

Downton station in Wiltshire, probably in the late 1950s, on the line that ran from Salisbury to West Moors. The station closed to passenger traffic and goods in 1964. (R.K.Blencowe)

Daggons Road station with its single platform opened in 1856. A dead-end siding at the station was converted to a loop in 1904 to facilitate shunting. (R.K.Blencowe)

Verwood on the Salisbury-West Moors line seen here in the 1950s. The station closed with the line in 1964, having lasted almost 100 years. (R.K.Blencowe)

All that remains of West Moors station today – the crossing keeper's cottage in Station Road. (Author)

protect a stylish hat, as shouting, 'It's like VE Day all over again!'

For many the night did not end with the last journey. The Carnival Queen and her attendants, the members of the Camera Club and members of the station staff were invited to a wine and cheese supper at the Fighting Cocks at Godshill. At 3 pm the next afternoon there was a strange occurrence. Many folk in Fordingbridge claimed that they heard an engine's whistle and a familiar chugging noise. Yet nobody actually saw 'the train' and the authorities denied its existence. Possibly for some the celebrations of the previous evening had lasted longer than expected!

At Fordingbridge today there is hardly a trace of the station which was sited to the west of the town although Station Road and Station Garage remain in evidence. At Breamore the station

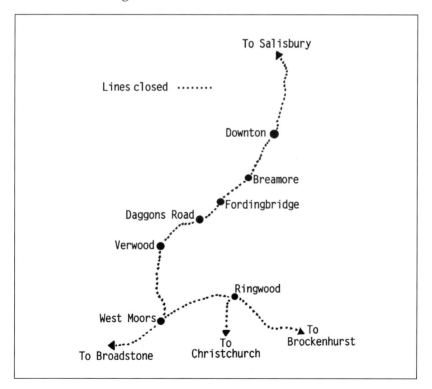

has survived the years. When visited by the author in September 2000, the 87-year-old wife of Leslie Trim, known as 'Dinky' Trim, still lived in the adjacent stationmaster's house. The late Leslie Trim was at one time in charge of Breamore station and he had resided at the stationmaster's house since the early 1940s. On the small platform were signs where a signal box had stood, once part of a building now derelict. After closure the nearby goods building became for a time a depot for United Dairies although a later owner specialised in walnut furniture.

At Daggons Road the station building has been demolished to become a bungalow and two houses – appropriately called Railway Cottages. The station was close to the village of Alderholt which, during the First World War, often had unexpected visitors when soldiers arrived by mistake instead of at their intended destination, Aldershot. Verwood station has gone but a road bridge survives close to the Albion Inn.

Southampton/Brockenhurst/Ringwood/ Broadstone

On 21st July 1845, the Southampton & Dorchester Railway obtained Parliamentary approval to build a line from South-ampton Central (then known as Blechynden) to Dorchester via Brockenhurst, Ringwood, West Moors, Wimborne and Ware-ham. It was also intended that Poole (at the site known today as Hamworthy Goods) should be included in the route but the nature of the coastline made this difficult, so instead a short branch was agreed.

The company had been formed in 1844 by a Wimborne solicitor, Charles Castleman, with a public meeting held in May 1844 in Southampton. Castleman had been adamant from the start that the line could never survive on local traffic and he saw it only as a link in a trunk route to the west. The proposed line was surveyed by Captain W.S. Moorsom, an experienced railway engineer. The route chosen was intended to give

Brockenhurst station, April 1953, where trains left for Christchurch, Lymington or Ringwood on the line known as 'Castleman's Corkscrew'. (R.K.Blencowe)

maximum benefit to a rather sparse area so its path through the various low hills and estuaries west of Southampton became a tortuous one. Because of this the line acquired the nickname of 'Castleman's Corkscrew' or 'the Water Snake'.

Much of the route was across open heathland so opposition from landowners to the new railway proved minimal. Good progress was made and by May 1847 the line was ready. Public opening was due on 1st June 1847 and many festivities were organised. However, two days before the event there was a disaster when part of a tunnel along the route at Southampton collapsed.

Support to the tunnel arch was necessary and this was carried out with timbers – which meant that through passage was now not possible! The only way to get the required rolling stock to the western end of the tunnel was by road and when the opening date came some trains did run on the official day. Despite the setback, celebrations at Ringwood went ahead with shops

Locomotive 34060 runs light past Holmsley station in the 1950s. The station opened in 1847 as Christchurch Road but was renamed Holmsley in 1862. (R.K.Blencowe)

Ex-Southern Railway West Country class 4-6-2 no 34006 'Bude' heads an enthusiasts' special, May 1956, at Ringwood station. Ringwood was once part of a line from Brockenhurst to Dorchester intended as a trunk route to Exeter but it never became a major cross-country route. (R.K.Blencowe)

54

The Railway Hotel at Ringwood is all that remains to remind passers-by that a station once existed in the area, today lost to industrial development. (Author)

closing early and there was dancing on the green. Other celebrations along the route were cancelled and a celebration dinner due to be held at the Crown Inn, Ringwood, took place a week later on 8th June 1847. Full services eventually started on 6th August.

The route can best be described by following the line from Southampton. After negotiating a tunnel, the track almost immediately reached what is now Southampton Central (previously Blechynden). Travelling westwards as far as Redbridge the track curves south to reach Brockenhurst. Beyond, the line crossed open country to reach Holmsley (Christchurch Road until 1862), Ringwood, Ashley Heath Halt (opened in April 1927), West Moors (opened in August 1867), Wimborne, Broadstone (opened as New Poole Junction) and beyond.

Initially there were five trains each way daily from Southampton to Dorchester and these soon proved popular. A regular cattle market at Ringwood also guaranteed considerable addi-

Following the demolition of Ringwood station, a newly-built road was named Castleman Way after Charles Castleman, a Wimborne solicitor, who formed the railway company in 1844. (Author)

tional revenue. In 1848, a year after opening, the line was taken over by the L&SWR and Charles Castleman was given a seat on the board. In due course traffic increased sufficiently to a figure stipulated in the Act that allowed double track to be built. Work on this began in 1857 with completion on the whole section some six years later.

When the Beeching Plan of March 1963 was announced, a Transport Users Consultative Committee (TUCC) enquiry was held in Bournemouth both for the Brockenhurst/Ringwood/ West Moors/Broadstone line and the Salisbury/West Moors line which was also scheduled for closure. There was little public opposition and the end for both lines came on 4th May 1964. On the Ringwood route, passenger services were withdrawn throughout and the section between Brockenhurst and Ringwood closed completely. Ringwood continued to see freight workings from the Wimborne end of the line for some years but these too were later suspended.

In contrast the route between Southampton and Brockenhurst was not only retained but it prospered with electrification to Bournemouth completed in July 1967. In May 1988 electrification was completed to Weymouth. Today fast electric trains pass through Brockenhurst where once steam trains turned westwards to Ringwood. The curved path that remains is almost the only tangible reminder of the past.

Ringwood station was soon demolished. Today the site is part of an industrial estate and the road built along the station trackbed is called, of course, 'Castleman Way'. Elsewhere, road improvements have cut across parts of the trackbed, yet long sections remain as footpaths. The Burley to Lymington road (close to the A35) passes where Holmsley station existed. The station building became a tea room with meals or snacks available in what was once the station's waiting room.

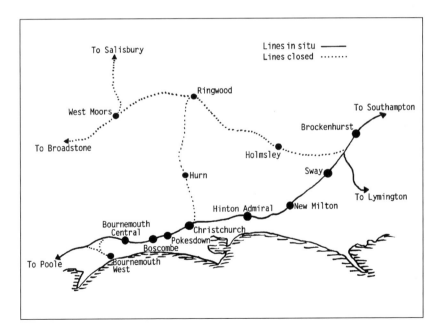

Ringwood/Hurn/Christchurch

With the Southampton & Dorchester Railway completed in 1847, access to Bournemouth for rail passengers meant travelling to Poole and then taking a rickety horse bus to complete the journey. For the inhabitants of Christchurch it was much the same. The nearest railway station was at Holmsley (opened as Christchurch Road) which required an 8 mile journey by horse-drawn coach over windswept heathland.

In the 7th September 1935 edition of *Christchurch Times,* an elderly resident reminisced over a journey to London in the late 1850s. A pony and trap had to leave Christchurch before daylight in order to catch a train at 9 am. Holmsley to London took five hours in railway coaches 'that were not built for comfort'. The local resident recalled, 'Ventilation was arrived at by a very crude method. One had to have the window either

Hurn station which opened in 1862 as Herne Bridge. Hurn was an intermediate station on the 7¾ mile branch between Ringwood and Christchurch. (Stations UK)

58

At the former Hurn station a C1 coach named the 'Avon Express' provides additional seating for the Avon Causeway Hotel which occupies the original station building. (Author)

open or closed. The combustion of the fuel for the engine was likewise crude, with the result that our faces and clothes were pitted with black coal smuts.'

A group of railway promoters considered that an approach by rail from Ringwood to Christchurch should be considered. The Ringwood, Christchurch & Bournemouth Company was formed and in 1859 powers were given to build a 7¾ mile line along the river Avon. The line, worked by the L&SWR, opened on 13th November 1862 with Christchurch becoming the railhead for Bournemouth. The route chosen was from a junction west of Ringwood, turning south through the New Forest and across land owned by Lord Egmont. Fortunately Lord Egmont was a keen supporter of the new railway and made no objection to the route crossing his land. All he requested in return was a private station at which trains would stop at his request. This was granted and a halt was constructed taking the name Avon

Christchurch station in the early 1930s. Note the advertisement offering Cadbury's Milk Chocolate at 2d. (Stations UK)

Lodge. The line had one other stopping place at Hurn which opened in November 1862. Initially this was known as Herne Bridge, it was renamed Herne in 1888 and became Hurn in 1897 which it remained until closure.

The contractors for the line had been Messrs Brassey & Ogling. Funds had been short and in order to keep costs down the track had been constructed across heathland and through pine forests, avoiding any earthworks that were considered unnecessary. Consequently, with so many severe gradients and curves, trains were restricted to a speed limit of 25 mph. For a line that was to carry trains from London and Southampton to the fast-growing resort of Bournemouth, the promoters had shown very little ambition.

Initially three trains daily passed slowly each way between Ringwood and Christchurch. As traffic to Christchurch and Bournemouth increased, the inconvenience of travelling on the time-consuming route via Ringwood became more apparent. In 1888 a direct route from Brockenhurst via Sway was opened to a junction at Christchurch where a new station was built. The original Christchurch station became part of the goods yard and the small engine shed was closed since the station was no longer a terminus and there was no need for such facilities.

It was soon apparent that the direct route via Sway would take all the traffic yet surprisingly the Ringwood/Christchurch branch remained in use for many years. Eventually on the evening of 28th September 1935, the last train to use the line left Bournemouth for Ringwood. The *Christchurch Times* reported, 'When services cease, Hurn station will close finally for all time. Its lights on the platform and in the signals will be extinguished and unbroken silence will descend upon the one-man station. The eight miles of track between Christchurch and Ringwood will be left to grass and rust. Maybe when the summer comes again the railway company will employ this length of rail to house some of their holiday homes – converted carriages let on hire to holiday-makers as summer bungalows.'

It seemed the greatest loss was to Mr H. Delia who had been acting stationmaster, chief clerk, ticket collector and porter at Hurn for the final eight years. He had no desire to leave Hurn where, reported the newspaper, he had 'lived happily in a cottage, if lonely at times. However, he has a dog for company'.

At Hurn station the former buildings have been converted into the Avon Causeway Hotel where many fascinating items of railway memorabilia can be found. At the entrance the original level crossing gates are still in existence and a C1 coach named the *Avon Express* stands alongside the former platform providing additional seating for meals. Although popular with visitors, the coach is perhaps not quite what Mr Delia, the acting station-master of 1935, imagined for the future.

4
A Line To Fawley And A Pier Railway

Totton/Marchwood/Fawley
Hythe Pier Railway

Marchwood station on the branch line to Fawley which opened in March 1925 and closed to passenger traffic in February 1966. (R.K.Blencowe)

Totton/Marchwood/Fawley

At a time when railways were approaching almost a century of development, the opening of a new line was somewhat unexpected. This was especially so in an area surveyed some years previously and considered unsuitable for rail traffic. But

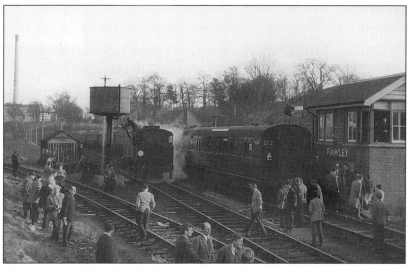

The terminus at Fawley which serves the nearby oil terminal. The terminus is photographed here after passenger closure and on the occasion of a visit by rail enthusiasts in a special train. (R.K.Blencowe)

commercial developments had taken place and 20th July 1925 saw the opening of the Totton, Hythe and Fawley Railway.

The 'waterside area', as it is known locally, had been surveyed for a railway at various times from about 1870 onwards. Several plans were put forward for lines, with one even contemplating a tunnel under the Solent to connect with the Isle of Wight. Not surprisingly such a plan failed to attract either investment or Parliamentary approval. But to the L&SWR, part of the scheme at least showed promise and, perhaps in an effort to test public opinion for a rail connection, the L&SWR instigated a bus service basically along the route of the later railway from 13th August 1906. The service lasted just over two years.

What was not widely known at the time was that in 1903 the L&SWR had already obtained the necessary powers for railway construction, possibly to thwart any later attempt by a rival company. When the bus service was abandoned it seemed as if the railway company was having second thoughts about the

Marchwood level crossing and station, May 2000. Today the line remains open for freight only, also with much revenue gained from the nearby Marchwood Military Port. (Author)

whole venture and, from November 1908 onwards, public transport to the area almost ceased.

In 1921 an independent company revived the scheme and the proposal was taken over by the new Southern Railway Company in 1923. Construction commenced and continued apace at an estimated cost of £250,000 for the 9 miles of railway. The new line was classed as a Light Railway meaning that, provided trains did not exceed 25 mph, economies could be applied with regard to level crossings and other works. The idea was to reduce costs both in construction and operation to a minimum.

As the name implies the line ran from a junction immediately west of Totton station, then turned almost at right-angles to run parallel with Southampton Water through the intermediate stations of Marchwood and Hythe to a terminus at Fawley. This was the site chosen by the Agwi Petroleum Company for its refinery. With a deep-water anchorage nearby it was the ideal location and rail communication was obviously part of the original plan. The Agwi Company later became part of the Esso group.

From the start the Southern Railway operated and staffed the line. A single track led off the main line with, at the time, no intermediate crossing places before the terminus. Station buildings were austere and functional. The Southern's love of concrete was indulged to the full, which was perhaps not always easy on the eye. Nevertheless each of the stations had 350 foot platforms and the usual facilities.

It was of course primarily refinery traffic that was handled, although as time passed extra revenue was obtained from the Marchwood Military Port and various commercial organisations, principally at Fawley. The former also possessed a large railway network within the confines of the port.

Over the years the importance of petroleum-based products continued to rise, so that by the mid-1950s the line was almost unable to cope with the traffic emanating from the refinery. Furthermore trains of empty tank wagons needed to be worked back to Fawley between the passenger trains, causing considerable congestion. Meanwhile the passenger service was very badly patronised. Accordingly extra line space was generated at Marchwood with a new loop installed in 1961, while in 1958 a halt was erected at Hardley in the hope of attracting additional passengers. Hardley Halt was short-lived, though, for on 14th February 1966 passenger services were withdrawn, leaving the whole route available for refinery and freight traffic.

Since then further changes have occurred with an underground pipeline carrying much of the finished product. But the railway certainly survives and its future seems secure. Every so often a request is made for the reinstatement of passenger trains to what is now a well-populated area. Time will tell if rail passengers will once again travel the line.

When visited in May 2000, proposals were being put forward to convert a large area of land adjacent to the track between Eling junction (on the main Bournemouth line) and Marchwood to a Freightliner Depot. Known as the Dibden Bay Development Plan, this has met considerable local resistance. A visit to

The former Hythe station on the Fawley branch photographed in May 1971. Over the years since closure in 1966 attempts have been made to have the station reopened for passengers but to date without success. (R.K.Blencowe)

Marchwood station showed it was virtually intact with its semaphore signals and level crossing gates close by. Hythe station's platform edge was found to be screened off by a wire fence but proposals have been considered to convert the station building into a visitor centre with displays including wildlife in the New Forest.

Hythe Pier Railway

Whilst at Hythe, a visit to the railway on the 700 yard long pier stretching into Southampton Water is recommended. When opened in 1880 its purpose was (and still is) to carry passengers and their luggage from the Southampton ferry across the river Test. Originally hand-propulsion along the 2 foot gauge track was used but after the First World War the owners decided to

A narrow gauge railway serves ferry passengers from Southampton on the 700 yard Hythe Pier. The line opened in 1880 and was electrified in 1922. (Author)

This Brush electric locomotive, currently in use on Hythe Pier, is one of three built in 1917 and purchased secondhand from the Avonmouth Mustard Gas Factory. (Author)

67

When visited by the author in May 2000, this pre-First World War coach was being restored as nearly as possible to its original colours. It will also carry the letters HPR (Hythe Pier Railway). (Author)

convert to a third-rail electric system. This was fed with a 200 volts DC supply taken directly from the local generating station.

Three Brush locomotives were purchased secondhand from the Avonmouth Mustard Gas Factory. The locomotives had originally run on 100 volt Exide batteries but when supplied to Hythe Pier the batteries were removed and two were fitted with collector shoes. The third was dismantled to provide spares. Apparently the original 5½ hp motors were never rewound and they continued to run quite satisfactorily on twice their intended voltage!

The pier reopened with its electric service in 1922 and not only continues to operate to this day but looks to the future. During the summer of 2001 it is planned that a pre-First World War coach will have been renovated and restored as nearly as possible to its original colours and also carry the letters HPR (Hythe Pier Railway).

5

Winchester To Alton And A Preserved Railway

Winchester/Alresford/Alton
The Mid-Hants Railway

Onlookers enjoy train-spotting at Alton station, c1923, as a train awaits departure to Winchester. (Stations UK)

Winchester/Alresford/Alton

The 17 mile gap between Alton and Winchester is dominated by a rise of the chalk uplands near Alton and the valley of the river Itchen at Alresford. During the 1860s such territory was hardly likely to attract a railway speculator. But, perhaps fuelled by

69

Medstead and Four Marks station photographed in 1964 on the Mid-Hants line which closed to regular passenger traffic in 1973. (Stations UK)

success elsewhere, a scheme was eventually proposed which resulted in the Alton, Alresford and Winchester Railway Company Act of 1861. With trains having reached Alton from Farnham in 1852, the shareholders saw the opportunity to provide a useful through line, giving trains from the capital to Southampton a shorter route than that through Basingstoke. It was thought unlikely that the Alton to Winchester line could rely on profit from rural traffic alone.

Construction took almost four years, a long time considering the terrain was all chalk. The line opened on 2nd October 1865, running from Alton to a connection with the main line two miles north of Winchester. The L&SWR staffed and operated the line from the outset. One goods and four passenger trains ran on weekdays only between Guildford and Southampton via the new route. The Alton-Winchester section of the journey took one hour, later reduced to 47 minutes after the settling of the earthworks. The track rose to 630 feet between Alton and Ropley, giving the line its 'Over the Alps' nickname. The highest point

70

was at Medstead station, making it the highest in Southern England.

This was hardly the service the directors had envisaged. Although it was possible to travel direct from Waterloo to Southampton via Alton, the journey time was upwards of an hour longer than the route via Basingstoke. It was hardly surprising that, with traffic failing to develop as anticipated, the 'Mid-Hants Railway' eventually gave up and sold out to the L&SWR in 1876.

There were originally three intermediate stations. Itchen Abbas served one of many villages clustered within a short distance of the railway. At Alresford the station was some way from the original town, prompting the independent development of New Alresford. Ropley station served a very large sprawl of hamlets and cottages. Medstead station was a later addition and was renamed Medstead and Four Marks from 2nd October 1937. Regrettably for the local population, repeated requests for a halt at Springvale to serve what was a rapidly growing community fell on deaf ears.

The line was single track throughout with passing loops at each station. The optimistic directors had anticipated future expansion and all the earthworks and bridges had been built to take double track. This is recognisable today, for the wide clearances provided by the various bridges are still apparent. Receipts were generally poor, although a considerable amount of traffic was generated by the watercress industry at Alresford. At its peak in the 1920s and 1930s, this involved several wagonloads daily. In addition there was a large grain store adjacent to Alresford station, which handled produce from the many arable farms in the area. At the other stops regular traffic was light, but enough to support each station at a time when almost everything bought on the domestic market arrived at the local station by train. Each station boasted its own stationmaster, clerk, porters and signalman. In addition there was a regular carter's service, the forerunner of today's parcel delivery.

History does not record any major accidents befalling the line over the years, although as would be expected irregularities did occur. One of these took place towards the end of December 1927

Locomotive 34020 hauling a passenger train enters Alresford station in 1953. The Mid-Hants line was single track throughout except for passing loops. (R.K.Blencowe)

when, following a sudden change in the weather, the countryside was engulfed by a blizzard. By 27th December the railway became impassable, with drifts up to 35 feet deep. Unfortunately this situation was discovered the hard way, as one newspaper of the period recorded: 'The 7.46 a.m. Eastleigh to Waterloo (via Alton) passed onto the single line at Winchester junction and disappeared.'

The luckless train was almost completely buried in a cutting near Itchen Abbas with just the top of the engine chimney visible. Normal passenger and goods workings did not resume until 4th January 1928.

By the end of 1957, steam on the line had given way to diesel. The new 'Hampshire' diesel units provided an hourly service in each direction from Alton to Southampton Terminus. The railway was also valued as an alternative route whenever the main line was for any reason not available. Thus the prestige express trains of the period, including the all-Pullman

Itchen Abbas station (photographed May 1950) was built to a unique design used exclusively by the independent Mid-Hants Railway. The station incorporated the stationmaster's living accommodation shown on the left. (R.K.Blencowe)

Bournemouth Belle, could occasionally be seen passing through what were usually quiet wayside stations.

Such visits ceased with the electrification of the Bournemouth line in July 1967, because the Mid-Hants route failed to feature in the modernisation proposals. As an electric service was available from both Alton and Winchester, the Mid-Hants railway was isolated.

For those associated with the railway the future was bleak and the eventual posting of closure notices in 1967 heralded the start of what was certainly the most vigorously fought anti-closure campaign the county has ever seen. It dragged on for several years but by late 1972 it was all over. On a cold Sunday night in early February 1973 the last train ran 'Over the Alps' to Alton. The end was not a wholly solemn occasion. In the expectation that throngs of people would gather to make the final journey, British Rail provided a main-line engine with several coaches

The platform at Itchen Abbas station (October 1971) looking towards Alresford. After closure the station was totally demolished to make way for a small area of houses. (R.K.Blencowe)

instead of the usual local diesel unit. Some of the civic dignitaries failed to recognise this as their train and were left stranded on the now-deserted platforms with what promised to be an eternal wait for the next train.

Little remains of the Alresford to Winchester junction section. The one intermediate station of Itchen Abbas has gone and only isolated concrete posts suggest a station might have been there at all. Yet with the newly-built houses having names such as 'Beeching', 'Station Lodge' and 'The Down Side', there really couldn't be much doubt.

The Mid-Hants Railway

When it had been known that closure was a certainty, two schemes were formed to try to save the line. These merged in

Alresford station, May 2000, headquarters of the restored Mid-Hants Railway. After closure of the original line in February 1973 it was to be another 12 years before trains could run again between Alresford and Alton. (Author)

May 1973 to form the Winchester and Alton Railway Company, supported by the Mid-Hants Railway Preservation Society. After lengthy negotiations with British Rail and various local authorities, a share issue was launched in May 1975. The aim was to provide a daily service of diesel rail cars from Alton to Winchester junction and an Alton-Alresford tourist steam railway. Response to the share offer proved disappointing and a second share issue which followed in November 1975 was aimed at a steam service only between Alton and Alresford.

This second issue was successful and proved to be the starting point of the Mid-Hants Railway as it is known today. Cash available made possible the purchase of the trackbed from Alresford almost to the BR station at Alton and an initial payment towards purchase of the track from Alresford to Ropley. BR removed the remainder of the track from Ropley to

Ropley station on the Mid-Hants preserved line. As the original Mid-Hants line was run down, Ropley became unstaffed from January 1967, to finally close to regular passenger traffic on 5th February 1973. (Author)

Signal box B at Ropley on the preserved Mid-Hants line. The station was also noted for its topiary, a good example still existing today. (Author)

A historic moment when the first official train of the Mid-Hants Railway leaves Alton for Alresford behind N class no 31874 on 25th May 1985. (Mike Esau)

Alton although fortunately this was after delivery of much of the Preservation Society's rolling stock. Since the Alresford to Winchester junction track was also removed about this time, the new Mid-Hants Railway was now isolated.

The new line began between the existing stations of Alresford and Ropley using the track that was still in place. When all was ready, after much feverish activity, the first official service began on 30th April 1977. The Chairman of Hampshire County Council was present to cut the tape and declare the line reopened, after which N class locomotive no 31874 hauled the first train.

All was now activity to establish the railway and prepare to extend back to Alton. More locomotives arrived, many from the Barry scrapyard requiring considerable restoration. Since any links with BR metals had gone, all the engines and carriages had

77

A train hauled by 2-6-2T ex-LMS Ivatt tank locomotive class 2MT arrives at Alresford in May 2000 on the preserved Mid-Hants 'Watercress Line'. (Author)

to be brought in on road vehicles. Activity remained at a high level and by early 1980 a £32,000 debt to BR could be paid off. By now the Preservation Society had become the largest shareholder and plans for expansion could be speeded up. Later in 1980, the Society was able to pay BR £23,000 to alter the layout at Alton station so that Mid-Hants trains could be accommodated on platform three. At about the same time, Medstead and Four Marks station, which had been badly vandalised, was restored to a workable condition. The final goal was in sight.

Track relaying took place in 1982 and 1983 and this was a totally volunteer operation. Many gave up their summer holidays to become part of the quest to reach Alton. On 28th May 1983 the first train reached Medstead and Four Marks station. The volunteers did not pause for long and, after considerable preparation, work on the final stretch to Alton began in March 1984. Much of the trackwork was done in

Locomotive 41312 (built in 1952) runs round a passenger set at Alresford before returning 'Over the Alps' to Alton. (Author)

appalling weather during the winter of 1984/5 but by April 1985 the task was complete. All concerned could indeed congratulate themselves when the first train, again hauled by N class 31874 (now renamed *Brian Fisk),* reached Alton from Alresford on 25th May 1985.

Today the 'Watercress Line' remains a flourishing private railway and a mecca for steam enthusiasts from all over the country. The connection with British Rail at Alton continues to give the project a new dimension and has ensured that the ride 'Over the Alps' is no longer just a memory.

6

The Bishop's Waltham Branch

Botley/Durley/Bishop's Waltham

The Bishop's Waltham branch opened in 1863 mainly to serve an adjacent brickworks and a wagon works. During much of the branch's life, a single railcar operated a shuttle between the terminus and Botley. (Stations UK)

There were few short dead-end rail branches in Hampshire. Railway speculators were wary of investing in any line which appeared to depend totally upon the development of one town. Such caution was well founded, for the short 3½ mile Bishop's Waltham branch was a typical example, lasting for passengers only until the early 1930s.

The railway, branching from Botley on the Bishopstoke (later

Botley station on the Fareham-Eastleigh line, until 1933 the junction for trains to Bishop's Waltham. The name board in this 1952 photograph suggests that 'Change for Bishop's Waltham' has been removed. (R.K.Blencowe)

Eastleigh)-Fareham line, was authorised in 1862 and absorbed by the L&SWR the following year. There were plans for an extension to Droxford on the Meon Valley line and on to Petersfield on the Portsmouth line. Another line was proposed to Ropley on the Mid-Hants line but none of these was ever carried out.

The route from Botley to the single-platform terminus was short, passing through the hamlet of Wangfield before reaching Durley. No heavy engineering works were needed during construction and few bridges were necessary. By contrast some eight private level crossings were required, to give access to areas of land divided by the new railway. It transpired that some of these crossings were little used and a survey of 1930 recorded that one had not been used for at least six years.

The branch opened to traffic on June 1st 1863, following the Hamble river to Bishop's Waltham. But the appeal of the branch to the railway promoters was that there was more than just the

81

Bishop's Waltham station closed to passenger traffic in 1933 but survived for goods traffic until 1962. In this 1953 photograph an RCTS special headed by class M7 locomotive 30110 brings rail enthusiasts to the terminus. (John H. Meredith)

usual traffic to be carried to and from a quiet country town. Bishop's Waltham was the site of a large brick and pottery works owned by Mr Blanchard. Its products were well known and it was considered that the industry could develop if improved transport became available.

Apart from the brickworks traffic the branch carried a variety of other freight, such as products from nearby lime kilns and coal for the town gasworks. Bishop's Waltham was one of the first towns in Hampshire to benefit from a piped gas supply. Shunting at the terminus, however, was always a long-drawn-out affair, for a locomotive had to run through a small engine shed in order to reach the other end of its train.

The terminus itself, built in Italianate style, was wooden-framed and decorated with red and yellow bricks in diagonal chevron patterns. The roof was part tiled and part slated. The building was designed to show to the best advantage the

Bishop's Waltham in 1953. Today a roundabout has taken the place of the station which was totally demolished after closure. (Stations UK)

products of the nearby brick and tile works. The terminus was rather unfortunately sited on the far side of the main Winchester to Portsmouth road. It is thought likely that the station was so placed to cater for the planned but unfulfilled extension to Droxford and Petersfield.

In addition to Mr Blanchard's works there was also a concern known as the Bishop's Waltham Wagon Works, although history fails to record if this company produced rail or road wagons. When some 20 years later in the 1880s the L&SWR was debating the site of a new carriage works, the Bishop's Waltham Town Council offered the town as a candidate but the suggestion was not taken up.

Market days in Bishop's Waltham were always busy times. To meet demand, rail services were, in later years, taken over by a steam railcar providing a shuttle service between Botley and the terminus. A private siding had been established at Durley Mill and in 1910 a short wooden platform was erected for the workers and local residents. Durley Mill attracted little trade traffic and the station, known as Durley Halt, attracted very few passengers, possibly because it was situated about a mile from the village. Despite this the platform remained open until the branch closed.

The depression of the 1930s meant the end for passenger traffic on what can only be described as an almost forgotten Hampshire branch line. The passenger service was unceremoniously withdrawn on 3rd January 1933, although receipts from freight were sufficient to maintain a thrice-weekly goods service for some years to come. A disadvantage for passengers had been that for those wishing to travel to Winchester or Southampton, it had been necessary to change at Botley and at Eastleigh.

Freight traffic came to an end on 30th April 1962. The closure was partly accelerated by the level crossing over the then main road from Winchester to Portsmouth (now the B2177) which caused considerable delays. Against the road transport network, the railway stood no chance. One of the last trains to carry any passengers was a special run on 27th April 1962. It was hauled by Ivatt class 2 tank locomotive 2-6-2 no 41328 running bunker first. It left Bishop's Waltham to a fusillade of detonators, hooting vigorously at crossings.

By the end of 1965 the station had gone and the track had been lifted. There had been hopes that the Hampshire Narrow Gauge Railway would replace the branch with a 2 foot gauge line but this was not to be. Today a roundabout has taken the place of the railway station at Bishop's Waltham and there is no trace of the brickworks. Only a solitary level crossing gate can be found together with a short section of track. But the gate did not come from the Bishop's Waltham branch, it came from Crow in the New Forest and the track was supplied by a scrap metal dealer. Also the photograph portraying a locomotive with a large bunker is inaccurate. It is representative of engines which, when rebuilt, worked the lines on the Isle of Wight!

7
The Railways Of Gosport

Bishopstoke/Fareham/Gosport/Clarence Yard
Fareham/Fort Brockhurst/Stokes Bay
Fort Brockhurst/Lee-on-the-Solent

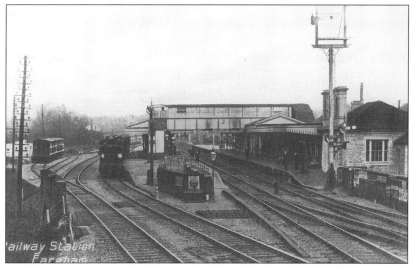

Fareham station in earlier steam days, photographed looking towards Eastleigh. Earlier last century Fareham was a busy junction with trains to Gosport, Stokes Bay and Lee-on-the-Solent plus a branch to Alton. (R.K.Blencowe)

Bishopstoke/Fareham/Gosport/ Clarence Yard

In the 1830s there were proposals for a line from Bishopstoke (renamed Eastleigh in 1923) to Portsmouth. These suggestions

85

*A passenger train headed by ex-L&SWR Drummond class T9 no 30289
awaits departure at Gosport station on 15th November 1952. Gosport station
opened in November 1841 but had to close shortly afterwards for two months
because of a landslip. (John H. Meredith)*

were vetoed by the Admiralty at an early stage but, on the other
side of the harbour, Gosport was far more receptive to the new
form of transport. Accordingly the London & Southampton, later
the L&SWR, built a line to the town via Fareham. The 15¾ mile
branch opened on 29th November 1841. It closed after only four
days since a tunnel at Fareham was considered unsafe and it did
not reopen until 7th February 1842.

To suit the optimism of the railway company, the architect
William Tite designed a massive Gosport station with arrival and
departure platforms fronted on one side by an equally
impressive stone colonnade. The total cost was put at just over
£10,000, compared with just £1,250 spent on each of the other
stopping places at Botley and Fareham. Unfortunately in their
haste to reach the town the promoters accepted a site for the
station which was some little way from the commercial centre.
Furthermore since the old walled fortifications of the town were

The most notable feature about Gosport station was its colonnade designed by Sir William Tite. It was intended to be an exact replica of that provided at Nine Elms terminus. This photograph was taken in May 1953.
(John H. Meredith)

still considered essential, Portsmouth Harbour being a heavily-defended naval base, the terminus had to be sited some ½ mile or so from the ferry pontoon which afforded connection with Portsmouth.

In those early days rail travel was very different to the experience of today. At Gosport passengers were summoned to the station at departure time by the loud ringing of a bell, whereupon they would enter their names and destinations in a book. From this the term 'Booking Office' later came about. The traveller was also forbidden to enter or leave a carriage. Railway regulations stipulated that a member of staff must assist and a veritable army of porters would attend every train.

Soon after the Gosport line opened it was patronised by Queen Victoria, making one of her first journeys by train on the occasion of the visit of Louis of France to England. In due course,

Ex-L&SWR Drummond class M7 0-4-4T no 30051 awaits departure with two coaches at Fareham, probably early 1950s. (R.K.Blencowe)

following the Queen's acquisition of Osborne House on the Isle of Wight, Royal trains became an almost regular feature of operation. Partly to placate Her Majesty an additional short connection was provided from the station into Clarence Yard. A private station was erected for the use of Royal travellers, although it is said the Monarch never used its waiting room.

Being a compact locality the Gosport area was one of the first to acquire a tramway system. A horse-drawn service commenced in the early 1880s and electric trams followed in 1906. The tramway extended through to Fareham in direct competition with the railway, which was not equal to the challenge.

With the outbreak of the Second World War the railway was given a new lease of life. Much of the traffic handled was destined for the various naval establishments dotted around the area. Unfortunately the strategic importance of the location was not lost on the enemy and one night early in 1941 Gosport station was almost totally destroyed by explosive and incendiary

Gosport station not long before closure in 1953. The station and the surrounding area suffered badly during the Second World War particularly when the station was almost totally destroyed by incendiary and high explosive bombs. (R.K.Blencowe)

Gosport goods yard May 1953. Enthusiasts from an RCTS special hauled by locomotive 30110 take photographs in the goods area. (John H. Meredith)

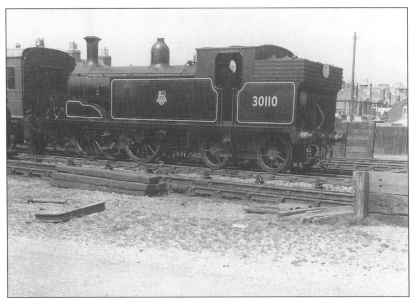

Ex-L&SWR Drummond class M7 0-4-4T no 30110 hauls an RCTS special at Gosport on 3rd May 1953, a month before closure of the line to passengers. (John H. Meredith)

bombs. Freight was still the main priority for the railway at the time so it was this side of the business that was restored first, passengers having little or no accommodation in which to shelter from the elements. The rival trams and buses then had the upper hand, a situation they exploited to such advantage that the railway closed to passengers on 8th June 1953, surviving for goods traffic until 1969.

Fareham/Fort Brockhurst/Stokes Bay

A short 1¾ mile branch from Fort Brockhurst (opened 1865/6 as Brockhurst) on the line to Gosport to a pierhead at Stokes Bay opened on 6th April 1863 for Isle of Wight passengers. The

Fort Brockhurst station south of Fareham where tracks separated to either Lee-on-the-Solent or Gosport and Stokes Bay. (R.K.Blencowe)

railway enabled passengers to step direct from train to steamer which, for Victorian families laden with luggage and children, must have been a boon. The double track line was not considered to be a branch line, but rather an extension to be used by through trains from Waterloo. To complete the line, numerous obstacles had to be overcome. In addition to the pier, two creeks and two moats had to be crossed but the main delays were caused by negotiations with the Admiralty and the War Office as well as the problems of raising sufficient money.

Stokes Bay pier could only take one train at a time since the track on the pier was single. There were platforms on either side of the track but no provision for the locomotive to run round the train. This problem was overcome by reversing the train to a nearby embankment equipped with double track and a signal box. The service never achieved great popularity because the pier was exposed to south-westerly winds and the service was

91

frequently cancelled. The pier was rebuilt in 1896 which eased the situation but did not solve the problem.

The branch's worst blow was when the railway on the Portsmouth side extended down to the Portsmouth Harbour in 1876. With these trains providing a faster service, the end became inevitable. Stokes Bay steamers were eventually withdrawn in the summer of 1914 but the railway survived for a time with passengers spending time on the beach. When the First World War commenced, naval activity in the area greatly increased and, not unexpectedly, the passenger service was withdrawn in November 1915.

In 1922 the pier was purchased by the Admiralty. The railway passenger service was never reopened and much of the line was removed by the Southern Railway in 1929. In the late 1930s a prospective builder concreted over the site of the track and built houses on either side. The pier continued to serve the Admiralty, mainly for loading torpedoes from standard gauge trolleys onto torpedo boats and aircraft which came from the Fleet Air Arm base at Lee-on-the-Solent.

Fort Brockhurst/Lee-on-the-Solent

Not far from Gosport is the resort of Lee-on-the-Solent which was reached by a short branch from Fort Brockhurst station opening on 12th March 1894. It was worked by a contractor until taken over by the L&SWR in 1909. The branch was built on a shoestring, with sharp curves and steep gradients to reduce to a minimum the earthworks required and consequent cost. The platform at Fort Brockhurst was built on the back of the L&SWR station so there was no direct connection with the Fareham to Gosport line. Wagons were transferred by means of a double shunt, thus avoiding the cost of points giving direct access to the main branch.

Fort Brockhurst, between Gosport and Fareham, was origin-ally known simply as Brockhurst. The change of name was

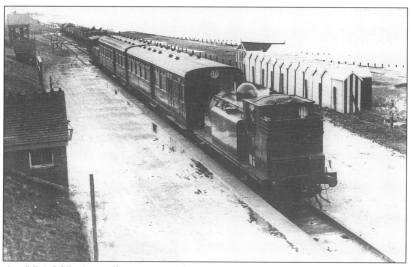

An LB&SCR Stroudley 0-4-2T class D1 seen here at Lee-on-the-Solent on 31st December 1930, the day the line closed to traffic. (R.K.Blencowe)

This is the site of the former Lee-on-the-Solent station, photographed almost 25 years after closure, where bathing huts have taken over. (R.K.Blencowe)

93

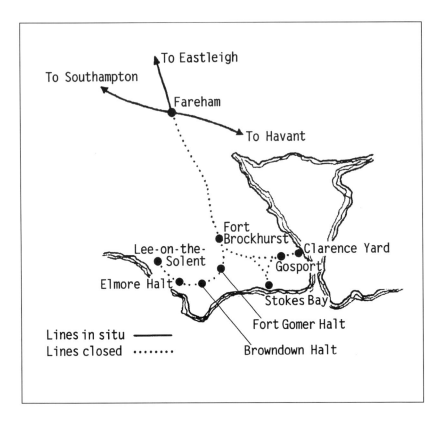

prompted by complaints from passengers for Brockenhurst whose luggage was sent down the Gosport line by mistake.

Before the First World War a service was maintained by just one rail motor-car. The railway company was frequently unable to meet its debts and by 1922 it owed some £14,000. The newly-formed Southern Railway was reluctant to take over the line or its debt particularly since Lee-on-the-Solent had become a suburb of Gosport, well equipped with frequent bus and tram services. The branch could not compete but under a Railways Act of 1921 the Southern Railway was bound to take it over. By 1930 it was apparent that there was no future for passenger

94

services and they were withdrawn at the end of the year with freight lasting until 1935.

The last passenger train ran on 31st December 1930. The local press reported that there were only six men and one dog on board.

8
The Meon Valley Line

Alton/West Meon/Fareham

West Meon Viaduct c1956. The Meon Valley railway was a latecomer to Hampshire, opening throughout in June 1903. It took five years to build and it never proved economic. (R.K.Blencowe)

The Meon Valley line ran from Alton on the Mid-Hants line to Fareham on the main Eastleigh to Portsmouth line. It was built by the L&SWR, partly as a defence to keep out the GWR which had by then reached both Winchester and Basingstoke. It was also considered as an alternative route to Gosport, Stokes Bay and Portsmouth. The line was a comparative late arrival in Hampshire, opening throughout on 1st June 1903.

The line had taken five years to build, involving the use of

West Meon Viaduct, viewed here from track level, was optimistically built for double track. It consisted of four 56 foot steel spans resting on steel piers. After closure of the line it was removed for scrap providing 725 tons of steel. (R.K.Blencowe)

numerous steam excavators, locomotives, horses and, of course, navvies. The route had been laid out for speed, with gentle curves and easy gradients, all indicative of its intended use as part of a new main line to the coast. Between Privett and West Meon two tunnels and an impressive viaduct had been built and, in anticipation of the heavy traffic, provision had been made for double track although this was never constructed. It remained a single track line throughout its life. Platforms were built almost 600 foot long and capable of taking main-line trains but, despite such provisions, most of the traffic was to be a local service from Alton to Fareham. With the line open, certain of the through Waterloo to Gosport services were diverted to the Meon Valley route, although the citizens of Gosport had long since found it easier to travel via the harbour ferry and Portsmouth for a fast service to or from the capital.

Droxford station which also claimed to serve Hambledon although the village was some miles to the east. The Meon Valley line had little passenger traffic and it was mostly freight that kept it alive. (R.K.Blencowe)

Not far from the entrance to the former Droxford station is a pillar box carrying a plaque reminding passers-by of Sir Winston Churchill decision-making there in 1944. (Author)

A train approaches Privett station in 1955 not long before closure of the branch. At one time Privett had a signal box and a goods siding. (Stations UK)

Southwards from Alton there were five intermediate stations. These were Tisted, Privett, West Meon, Droxford and Wickham. Each was built in the same basic style and provided with commodious facilities and was capable of handling ten-coach trains. In addition there were a number of goods sidings. A goods depot at Mislingford, north of Wickham (unusually no passenger station was opened), handled large quantities of timber traffic from nearby woods. Another goods depot opened at Farringdon where in May 1931 a passenger halt was added.

According to *The Railway Magazine* of July 1933, the line found an unexpected use when a complete farm was moved by rail. On May 10th, the entire equipment and stock of Brockwood Park Farm near West Meon was moved to Stalbridge in Dorset in two Southern Railway trains. The stock included 50 sheep and lambs, 17 cows, 13 heifers and calves, 3 bulls, a goat plus a pony and foal, ferrets, dogs and pigeons. The only animal left behind was

Close to the A32 beyond a former road bridge can be found Privett station building and its platform. The station closed in February 1955 and the building is today a strictly private residence. (Author)

the farm cat which clearly took exception to the move.

As it might have been expected, the Meon Valley line proved an expensive route to maintain with the two long tunnels at Privett and West Meon as well as numerous chalk earthworks. But it was a picturesque line, the relaxing journey allowing ample time to enjoy the surrounding countryside. Engine crews too found the leisurely schedules to their advantage, for mushrooms grew wild in the fields alongside the railway. If a train was an unusually long time between stations the reason was often readily apparent. Years later when the line closed West Meon tunnel was for some time turned over entirely to the cultivation of mushrooms.

With little passenger traffic, it was freight that kept the line alive. A daily pick-up service was provided to collect the various wagons left for loading the previous day. Again it was a leisurely

Farringdon Halt on the Meon Valley line opened with the branch in June 1903. Photograph taken c1930. (Stations UK)

process, accompanied on occasions with home-made wine from one of the railway cottages after which work was liable to take longer! There was also a good deal of milk traffic which was taken by passenger train and destined for the London creameries.

As with so many lines it is for wartime events that the Meon Valley is perhaps best remembered. Evacuees arrived from Portsmouth, Gosport and Southampton to the relative safety of the countryside, only to be followed by enemy planes which managed to bomb West Meon village and station yard. Churchill and other Allied leaders are said to have formulated plans for D-Day in a coach at a siding at Droxford station and also at nearby Southwick House. A photograph of the VIPs at the station adorned the booking office for many years. A pillar box close to the station entrance still carries a plaque which reads:

In a special train at this station the Rt. Hon. Sir Winston Churchill M.P. then Prime Minister of the U.K. spent some

101

A goods train passes through Tisted station, c1923. The Meon Valley line was built as a 'blocking line' to thwart GWR attempts to reach the South Coast ports. (Stations UK)

days making crucial decisions with his staff, prior to the invasion of Europe on D. Day June 6th 1944

Local hearsay recalls an occasion when Mr Churchill met with President de Gaulle. Mr Churchill, recalling France's dubious role in the earlier days of the war, refused to meet President de Gaulle at the station and made the President walk some two miles to where Mr Churchill's coach was actually located.

Following the war, economy became necessary with the Meon Valley an early casualty, closing to passengers and through goods services in 1955. Two stubs of track, one from Alton as far as Farringdon and the other from Droxford to Knowle junction (on the main Eastleigh to Fareham line), survived for many years. The latter section acquired new life when Mr Charles Ashby of Southampton leased the track to experiment with a new design of railcar. The car was built by Strachans at Hamble, based on one of their luxury road-coaches. It had metal flanged

Tisted station on the Meon Valley line between Alton and Fareham closed in February 1955. Today it survives as a private residence complete with its platform and a C1 coach. (Author)

wheels with solid rubber tyres, a wheel base of 20 feet and an unladen weight of 6 tons. Its standard 9-litre engine could give a maximum speed of 70 mph with a fuel consumption of 11 miles per gallon. The car was destined for the Isle of Wight and Mr Ashby considered that the line from Droxford was typical of the line on which it would run. The railcar was called the *Sadler Pacerailer*. One night in 1970 vandals succeeded in setting fire to the car and what might have been a highly successful project came to an unhappy end.

But Mr Ashby had other interests. In addition to the railcar, he had acquired other items forming what could have been the beginnings of a preservation society. These included ex-LB&SCR Stroudley Terrier locomotive no 32646 plus Bulleid restaurant car no S7679S. Hopes for steam revival seemed encouraging. Nevertheless Mr Ashby decided to sell the Terrier to Brickwoods

103

On the side of the road bridge above Tisted's platform is this fine replica of the L&SWR emblem made by a previous owner of the station building. (Author)

Brewery on Hayling Island for use as a pub sign outside the Hayling Billy public house – see chapter 11. (*Hayling Billy* can be found today at the Isle of Wight Railway renamed *Freshwater* and renumbered '2'.) But steam hopes were kept alive when the Terrier was replaced by USA 0-6-0 tank locomotive no 30064.

In January 1970 connection with the main line at Knowle junction was severed and what was left of the Meon Valley line became isolated. Before this happened locomotive 30064 together with numerous items of rolling stock were removed to Exchange Sidings at Liss prior to storage on the Longmoor Military Railway. Mr Ashby's hopes were finally dashed and by 30th May 1970 the Droxford to Knowle junction section was finally closed and the tracks were taken up.

Today much of the original railway has reverted to its former use as farmland with embankments ploughed over and cuttings

A train awaits departure at Wickham station, c1955. There were possibilities in the 1960s, after closure of the branch, that Wickham could have been a station on a preserved line but hopes were dashed when a connection with the Eastleigh-Fareham line was removed. (Stations UK)

refilled. At least one of the cuttings has been used as a rubbish dump before being finally covered with a layer of topsoil. North of Farringdon the route has been almost obliterated. Of what survives, the best preserved stretches are to be found between West Meon and Droxford, and south of Wickham. In both cases the trackbed has been turned into a nature walk.

A number of stations have been converted into attractive private residences. Tisted not only retains its railway character but a class C1 coach stands at the platform. In addition a L&SWR emblem, made by a previous owner of the station, proudly looks down from an adjacent road bridge. Privett station building has also become a private residence. At one time Privett had a signal box and a goods siding. The signal box closed in 1922 and became a ground frame. The signals were removed and after dark the only way engine drivers knew they were approaching

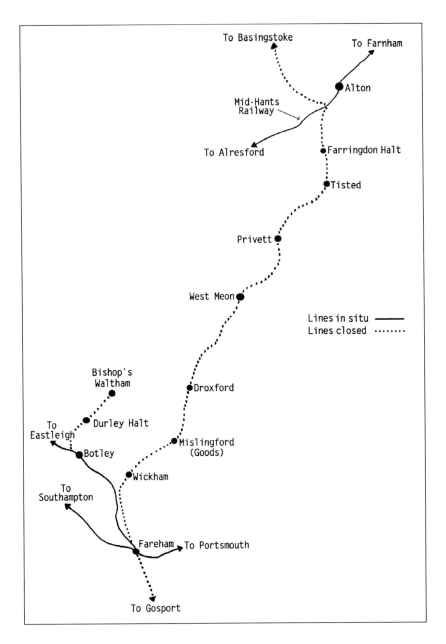

To Basingstoke

To Farnham

Alton

Mid-Hants
Railway

To Alresford

Farringdon Halt

Tisted

Privett

West Meon

Lines in situ ———
Lines closed ········

Bishop's
Waltham

Droxford

To
Eastleigh

Durley Halt

Mislingford
(Goods)

Botley

Wickham

To
Southampton

Fareham ► To Portsmouth

To Gosport

the station was by the use of marker lights. Droxford station building suffered badly from vandalism when untenanted in the 1960s but today it has reclaimed its former dignity complete with platform and awnings although the residence is strictly private.

Had the railcar venture of the 1960s succeeded then a preserved railway between Droxford and Fareham might well have proved highly successful. Sadly this was not to be.

9

A Cross Country Branch From Basingstoke

Basingstoke/Alton

Onlookers pose at Herriard station on the Basingstoke to Alton branch, c1930. Station buildings along the line were very primitive and all were some distance from the villages they purported to serve. (Stations UK)

Standing by a clump of trees near a row of cottages it seemed difficult to imagine that as recently as 70 years ago a light railway passed through on its route between Basingstoke and Alton. It seemed even harder to imagine that in a gap between the trees once stood Cliddesden station, a primitive building of wood and corrugated iron construction. But Cliddesden was more than a station on a little-used railway line. In 1937 it

Overgrown remains are all that are left of Cliddesden station photographed here in 1964. The station, which closed to passenger traffic in 1932, was used in the making of the Will Hay film 'Oh! Mr Porter' in 1937 when it was renamed 'Buggleskelly'. (Stations UK)

featured as the background to a Will Hay film called *Oh! Mr Porter* when it acquired the name of 'Buggleskelly' with Will Hay (supported by Graham Moffatt and Moore Marriott) coming there as a new stationmaster. Locomotives used in the film included Kent & East Sussex Railway's no 2 brought from Kent for the occasion and a former L&SWR express no 657 built at Nine Elms in 1895.

The branch from Basingstoke to Alton was one of the few light railways to be built in Hampshire. By conforming to certain legal criteria of an 1896 Act of Parliament, such as an overall speed restriction of 25 mph, a railway officially classed as 'light' was able to dispense with the expensive operating requirements that a normal railway was bound to observe by law.

The railway, a relatively late addition to the county network, came about primarily as a blocking line designed to thwart the advances of the GWR from Basingstoke. Approval for construc-

Railway cottages at Cliddesden, south of Basingstoke, on the Basingstoke and Alton Light Railway. The adjacent station of Cliddesden, now completely demolished, was 1½ miles from the village – almost as far as from Basingstoke! (Author)

tion was obtained under the 1896 Light Railways Act and the line opened to traffic on 1st June 1901. Between Basingstoke and Alton the line followed a curved path, with three intermediate stopping places, Cliddesden, Herriard and 'Bentworth and Lasham'. From about 1909 a small platform was added just outside Alton to serve the Lord Mayor Treloar Hospital.

Each of the three original stations was in the charge of a stationmaster, although really this man had to be a do-it-all person who frequently had to cope with tasks normally undertaken by other staff. The minimal traffic receipts were insufficient to support more than a single additional porter to assist the stationmaster. The railway provided accommodation for these men in cottages close to the stations. The position of stationmaster warranted a detached house while the porter and members of the track gang shared a group of terraced houses.

110

Bentworth and Lasham station became a coal yard after closure of the Basingstoke to Alton branch to goods traffic in 1936. (Stations UK)

Water to the station and the properties came by means of wind pumps which drew supplies from bore holes deep in the chalk.

Unhappily for the railway company, receipts did not meet the line's expenditure. As with some of the other Hampshire lines, an early attempt at economy was made in the form of steam railcar working. These devices, being essentially single carriages self-powered by small steam engines, did away with the need for separate locomotives. Unfortunately design failings often offset the expected benefits. This precarious existence continued until the time of the First World War when, at the end of 1916, the complete railway was unceremoniously closed and the rails taken up for use in transporting stores behind the front line in France.

From contemporary records it is apparent that the L&SWR quietly hoped the little line would soon be forgotten, although as a concession a daily lorry service was provided to transport milk and farm produce to the railhead at Basingstoke. However, the idea of closure was far from the minds of the landowners along the route, many of whom had openly supported the railway in the first place. In consequence there followed a long and hard-fought battle involving Parliament, with the L&SWR being accused of closing the railway without giving the required notice. Eventually the railway company conceded defeat, and gangs of men moved in to clear the overgrown trackbed and relay the track. By mid-August 1924 the trains were running again.

The 13 mile branch had been restored much as it was before, except that the passing loops were not relaid. This meant that only one train at a time could use the line. The timetable was also altered to allow it to be operated by one set of men who worked from Basingstoke, where the engine and carriages were based. There were now three trains in each direction daily and the early morning and late evening trains were discontinued. These arrangements did not meet with the approval of the farmers or the passengers, who felt they had been badly let down. There were now no separate goods trains, requiring the midday train each way to run as 'mixed' conveying goods as well as passenger traffic.

Other changes affected the stations. With the closure of the line in 1916 the stationmaster had been withdrawn, leaving the porter in sole charge. The same arrangement applied now that train services were restored. This lack of immediate control sometimes resulted in unexpected and unsupervised 'goings on'. On one occasion a game of cricket involving some of the menfolk from a nearby village caused the service to be forgotten – until the train proceeded to demolish the adjacent level crossing gates which had not been opened. Another time a pedal cycle arrived for delivery to a customer. The porter found it to his liking and so rode it round the village for some time, using it for the delivery and collection of parcels. Eventually it developed a puncture – whereupon it was promptly dispatched to the rightful owner.

For some the line is best recalled for its part in two classic films: *Oh! Mr Porter* has already been mentioned but another film was *The Wrecker*, made in 1928. The films contrived to show the

A short section of L&SWR track from the Basingstoke and Alton Light Railway has been preserved at the Basingstoke Viables Roundabout, to be found along Harrow Way to the south of the town. (Author)

line in two totally different roles, the first as a sleepy country branch line and the second as part of a main-line route involving a crash between a train and a lorry on a level crossing.

For *The Wrecker* Gainsborough Films purchased an engine and carriages from the Southern Railway. The train was set in motion, after which the driver jumped clear, leaving the engine to plough on towards almost certain destruction. Derailment of some sort was assured as numerous keys supporting the rails had been removed and a charge of dynamite added for good measure. Since it was a once-only take, the film-makers could only hope that the result would be sufficiently spectacular. The actual crash, filmed from several different locations, was a remarkable success. After the crash, actors entered the wrecked coaches (no doubt covered with tomato sauce . . .) to be 'rescued' later in the day.

During the late 1920s a slow but gradual escalation of operating expenses occurred, coinciding with an equivalent

113

decline in passenger and goods revenue as the use of motor vehicles increased. With perhaps one or possibly two passengers per train the line could not hope to survive and closure to passenger traffic came on 12th September 1932. Two short stretches were retained at each end. Treloar platform remained in use for the occasional special train as well as deliveries to the hospital until 1967, while just south of Basingstoke there was a siding serving the Thornycroft lorry works.

Very little of the line remains today. Although Cliddesden station has gone it is still possible to look towards Basingstoke where a line of trees and bushes clearly shows the path of the former trackbed. And adjacent to where the station stood, a line of former railway cottages can be seen. In Basingstoke itself, at the Viables Roundabout on the Harrow Way, a short section of track has been preserved in silent tribute to the light railway which lasted only 31 years.

10
The Longmoor Military Railway

Bentley/Bordon/Longmoor/Liss

Military personnel pose for a picture at Bordon station, September 1958. Bordon was one of numerous military camps in the area served by the Longmoor Military Railway (LMR). (R.K.Blencowe)

The military camps at Blackdown, Bordon and Longmoor, situated in the north-east of the county between Bentley and Liss, were initially constructed for troops returning from the Boer War. The areas became associated with railway construction and it was not long before some 4½ miles of 18 inch gauge double track with lines over 20 feet apart had been built

A passenger train arrives at Bordon hauled by locomotive 30027. The 4½ mile branch opened in 1905 between Bentley and Bordon to connect Bordon with the main line from Aldershot and Guildford. (R.K.Blencowe)

between the two camps.

The line's initial traffic must have proved quite a sight. The first goods to be pulled consisted of 68 army huts placed on trolleys running simultaneously on the parallel tracks hauled by steam winch, ploughing engines or horses. Troops were being moved from Longmoor to Bordon and it was decided this was the best way to tackle the problem!

Under a Light Railway Order of 1902, a standard gauge branch was constructed from Bentley on the Farnham-Alton line (which opened in 1852) to Bordon for the military camp. The 4½ mile line was built at a cost of just £30,000 following agreement between the L&SWR and the War Department. Funding came entirely from the L&SWR, convinced it could easily recoup the costs from the anticipated traffic.

The line opened in 1905 and in 1906 a halt was constructed to serve the village of Kingsley. Although sufficient land was purchased to develop a station and goods yard, this never

An excursion organised by the Railway Enthusiasts Club stops at Kingsley Halt, an intermediate station between Bentley and Bordon which opened in 1906. The halt comprised only a name board, a timetable board, a lamp-post and a seat. (Lens of Sutton)

Kingsley Halt on the Bentley-Bordon branch, April 1949. The train is hauled by ex-LMS M7 class 0-4-4T, still carrying its Southern Railway number and livery. (R.K.Blencowe)

117

Bordon, the terminus on the branch from Bentley, which served the nearby Bordon Military Camp. The branch closed to passenger traffic in 1957. (Stations UK)

happened. Kingsley remained one of the simpler halts with only a lamp-post, name board, timetable board and a seat. If it rained you got wet.

At about the same time the Royal Engineers started work on a standard gauge military line from Bordon to Longmoor. It opened in 1907 although some constructional work at Whitehill was not completed until 1910. The railway served a dual role, since it not only provided transport for men and stores to the various camps in the area but it also served as a railway training centre for Royal Engineers in case of need either at home or abroad. From 1908 the line was known as the Woolmer Instructional Military Railway.

The lines saw much military activity during the First World War and in the month of April 1915 alone special traffic at Bordon included 50 troop trains plus 8,000 soldiers. Towards the end of the war the line was able to prove its value in Europe. As

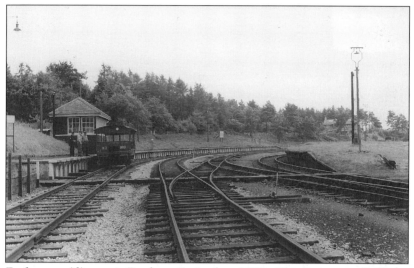

Exchange sidings at Bordon, September 1958. The Longmoor Military Railway was extended in the early 1930s to Liss to connect with the direct Portsmouth line. (R.K.Blencowe)

Allied troops advanced, many men put their training in railway practice to good use in Belgium and France.

After the First World War the line was allowed to be run down at a time when many other military railways were being closed. In 1933 however, rather unexpectedly, the Longmoor line was extended for about 3 miles southwards through Liss Forest to join the main Guildford to Portsmouth line at Liss although no physical connection was made until 1942. Traffic on the line was increasing once again and, in addition to the military, it served many civilians employed in the area. Many of such employees enjoyed the privilege of being conveyed free of charge although by a train service that was determined by a military programme rather than by traffic requirements. In 1933 the line became known as the Longmoor Military Railway (LMR).

Increases to route mileage and layouts continued. A circuit of track used for training known as the Hollywater Loop had been constantly laid and torn up. It was finally rebuilt and completed

WD locomotive LMR 400 runs round coaches at Liss, September 1958. The Longmoor Military Railway closed in 1969 but it will surely still be well remembered by many ex-military personnel. (R.K.Blencowe)

in 1943. This gave 6 miles of continuous running in terrain which proved suitable for all kinds of training.

During the Second World War the LMR provided instruction for as many as 27,000 men a year. The extra track mileage proved necessary for practice in building and repair techniques as well as operating methods. By 1943 the LMR had reached its peak with a track of 71 miles. As many as 27 passenger trains travelled daily from Liss to Longmoor with 19 going on to Bordon. Passengers carried rose to 3,650 daily and freight trains brought in nearly 500 wagons a day.

Many of the locomotives used were WD, built for the LMR. Although major overhauls were sent to Eastleigh, workshops locally dealt with the majority of running repairs. Some engines were acquired secondhand from the civilian railways while others were borrowed for short periods for training or testing purposes. Many designs could be seen including the massive

Schoolchildren wait on Bentley station platform on the line from Farnham to Alton, c1930. On the right the bay that served trains to Bordon. (Stations UK)

American-styled 2-8-0s. It was ironic that the sidings put to such good use during the war for locomotive servicing were to be used from 1945 to store locomotives made redundant.

After the war many other emergency railway training centres closed down and for a time Longmoor became the main centre for the British Army. As time passed even the LMR was slowly run down. The Hollywater Loop was closed and other sections followed. On 16th September 1957 the line from Bentley to Bordon closed its passenger service with all traffic ceasing by 4th April 1966. Before final closure of the LMR, however, interest in the line had been increasing and a series of successful open days were held when the public could travel on the trains. The culmination of these events came when the LMR gave permission to store a number of former BR steam engines which had been purchased privately following the end of steam locally in July 1967. At the time it was hoped these could form the nucleus of a private steam railway.

121

Bentley station between Farnham and Alton. The bay platform for trains to Bordon was on the far left where today trees have taken over. (Author)

With the closure of the Bordon line, the only access to the LMR was via Liss. The northern terminal of the LMR had become a wooden platform at Oakhanger near Bordon Camp. By 1969 the Ministry of Defence decided that, in the economic climate of the day, it could no longer afford the expenses of a military railway and a decision was taken to close. On 31st October 1969, special journeys marked the sad occasion with runs to Oakhanger and back. One such train was pulled by the majestic 2-10-0 no 600 *Gordon* pulling three saloons dating from 1909 to 1920 comprising L&NWR and L&SWR stock.

During its life, the LMR achieved popularity with film-makers who used the area to produce such films as *The Lady Vanishes* and *The Inn of the Sixth Happiness*. Another well-known film was *The Great St Trinian's Train Robbery* made in 1965. To achieve their ends, film-producers had diesel and steam trains carrying out operating practices that would hardly have received BR approval!

After closure, there had been hopes that the last mile or two of LMR track from Liss to Liss Forest together with the interchange sidings at Liss with BR might be saved so that a preservation society could be established. Despite the efforts of many dedicated enthusiasts and locomotive owners, such efforts were frustrated by the Liss Forest residents who were determined that this should not happen. The section of track had its last moment of glory when film-makers in 1972 moved in once more to shoot scenes for *Young Winston* recalling moments of the Boer War in Africa.

Today little remains of the once important railway. The preserved locomotives were moved to other sites and the site of Bordon station gave way to new development. Where the track once crossed Liss Forest, today a walk exists along part of the old trackbed. Yet surely the area will never be forgotten by the thousands of soldiers who passed through it during two World Wars.

11
Trains To Hayling Island

Havant/Hayling Island

A Hayling Island train waits for departure in a bay at Havant station. The 4½ mile branch closed in November 1963 having lasted 96 years. (R.K.Blencowe)

Hayling Island lies to the east of Portsmouth, an island only in the loosest sense of the word and then only at high tide. The idea of a railway to serve the area appealed to the local landowners and businessmen who saw their neighbours at Havant prospering on the trade brought by the LB&SCR railway which ran along the coast from Brighton to Portsmouth. Parliamentary powers were obtained in 1860 for a line from Havant to a terminus at South Hayling (renamed Hayling Island in 1892). Difficulties in obtaining finance, as well as arguments concerning the amount of compensation paid to the landowners along the

Ex-LB&SCR class A1X 0-6-0T no 32677 designed by William Stroudley at Hayling Island, May 1953. (John H. Meredith)

A Hayling Island train at Havant headed by a Stroudley Terrier waits at the branch platform, 1964. (Stations UK)

Langston, an intermediate station on the Hayling Island branch. (The station name was Langston whereas the Ordnance Survey marked the village as Langstone.) In 1882 a freight train ferry service was introduced between Langston and St Helens on the Isle of Wight but it survived only six years. (R.K.Blencowe)

route, delayed completion until 1867. Eventually, on 17th July of that year, the first trains were able to use the branch.

Initially the service was operated by the contractor who had built it, Frederick Furniss. This arrangement continued until 1st January 1872, when the LB&SCR took over operation on a temporary basis. A permanent lease was negotiated some two years later. From then on the short branch settled down to a regular pattern of operation. Receipts swelled during the summer months as gradually more and more visitors came to know of the line and took their holidays in the Hayling area.

Heavier locomotives could not be used because of the light construction of the bridge spanning that part of Langstone Harbour which cut off Hayling at high tide. Because of this trains were usually hauled by Terrier class locomotives weighing under 30 tons. Trains comprised no more than four 4-wheeled

Remains of the 1,100 foot wooden-trestled Langstone Harbour Bridge viewed from the southern abutment in October 1994. Note the higher bases for the swing bridge which spanned the central area. (John H. Meredith)

coaches lit by oil lamps. As there were no passing places on the 4½ mile single track branch, a regular 30-minute service was the maximum possible capacity.

Following the route from Havant the track wound its way through a shallow cutting and then opened out at the first stopping place, Langston Halt. For many years this was just a single wooden platform and shelter, until the Southern Railway provided concrete replacements. Next came a series of sidings to left and right, which provided direct loading and unloading facilities for the numerous vessels using the harbour. Changing transport patterns meant that the facilities were used less and less over the years.

The railway then crossed Langstone Harbour on a wooden trestle viaduct, some 1,100 feet long and 25 feet above high water level. In the centre was a 40 foot opening section, controlled from a small wooden signal box appropriately called Langstone

127

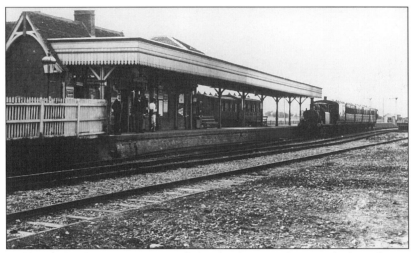

Hayling Island station, 1963. Before motor cars took over, the branch was popular with trippers and taxis were always available to take holiday-makers to nearby boarding and guest houses. (Stations UK)

The 10.52 am train to Havant awaits departure at Hayling Island station, 15th September 1952. The branch closed in November 1963, partly due to the poor condition of Langstone Bridge. (R.K.Blencowe)

After closure of the Hayling Island branch, Stroudley Terrier 32646 'Hayling Billy' was placed for a time outside the Hayling Billy public house. It can be found today at the Isle of Wight Railway, renamed 'Freshwater' and renumbered '2'. (Picture courtesy Isle of Wight Railway Company Ltd)

Bridge Box. The whole structure was carried on less than 50 trestles bedded in concrete. Such wooden structures were commonplace in the early days of railways, some of the most famous being the Brunel timber viaducts in Devon and Cornwall.

Having crossed the bridge trains then travelled along the foreshore to North Hayling Halt, just under 2½ miles from Havant. The halt was another wooden structure and somewhat exposed to the winds from the harbour. Its position was such that exceptionally high tides would bring flood water almost to track level.

Road and rail, which up to this point had run almost parallel, now parted. The railway followed the shoreline for a further 2

A Hayling Island Farewell special organised by the LCGB (Locomotive Club of Great Britain) headed by locomotive 31791 pauses at the Royal Naval Barracks platform at Portsmouth on 3rd November 1963. (John H. Meredith)

miles to the terminus station which, in the best railway tradition, was some little way from the actual town. The station building was of a substantial brick construction and provided with two platform faces. Improvements made by the Southern Railway in the 1930s included additional platform canopies and extra sidings, an indication of the increasing popularity of the resort.

Being primarily a holiday destination it was the summer months that saw the most traffic, the Terriers struggling with coachloads of holiday-makers – sometimes trains had to be double-headed. It proved on occasions to be a trying time for booking clerks who had to cope with an invasion of strangers, many with unfamiliar accents and asking for tickets to all manner of destinations.

Unfortunately these peaks of revenue were not matched by trade at other times, a situation which was hardly acceptable to a railway in the 1960s. March 1961, for example, saw only 2,000

The last public train on the Hayling Island branch, 3rd November 1963, organised by the LCGB. Locomotive 32636 heads the train with 32670 at the rear. The first coach was plastic-bodied and experimental. (John H. Meredith)

tickets collected at Hayling while in August the same year the figure was 32,000. It was clear such a situation could not continue and closure was eventually announced. Another reason given was the poor condition of the wooden viaduct, while delays caused to road traffic at the various level crossings were also considered unacceptable. The Hayling Island branch came to an end on 4th November 1963. We have already read (chapter 8) how, after closure, Stroudley Terrier 32646 *Hayling Billy* was placed for a time outside the Hayling Billy public house.

There were hopes that, after regular services had ended, passenger trains of some sort might be restored. Enthusiasts acquired electric tram cars and, for a time, a car from Blackpool Corporation could be seen travelling along the track. The idea did not succeed and the Blackpool car was transported to Lowestoft. Langstone Bridge was subsequently dismantled and

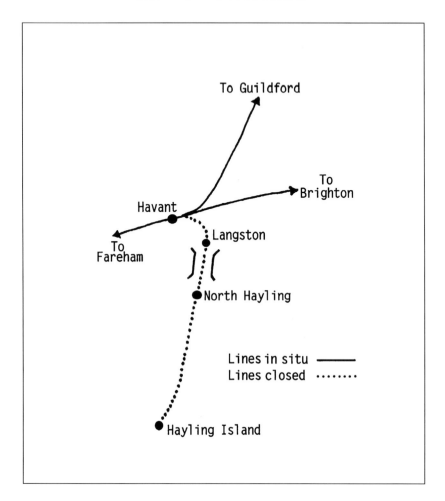

the remaining track slowly disappeared under a forest of weeds to be finally removed by a scrap merchant. The wooden halts were sold as firewood.

Today sections of the route have found a new use as footpaths, the ballast having been removed and replaced by grass. From a point to the north of the island the old trackbed has become the 'Hayling Billy Leisure Trail', ending appropriately at the Hayling

132

Billy public house in what is still called Station Road. Elsewhere housing has been built on much of the trackbed. At the site of Langstone Bridge it is hard to visualise today how the railway ever reached the island, although at low tide stumps of the viaduct reappear as if in gaunt tribute.

12
L&SWR Trains Into Sussex

Petersfield/Midhurst

Petersfield station on the Portsmouth Direct line, 1967. On the left the original 1859 gabled building has survived the years.

Had early railway planners had their way then Petersfield might have become an important junction with lines leaving the town in several different directions. First trains to reach Petersfield came on 1st January 1859 when a line (to become known as the Portsmouth Direct) was opened by the Portsmouth Railway Company from Farncombe to Havant. A further line was planned from Ropley on the Mid-Hants line, through to West Meon where tracks would go on to link with Bishop's Waltham and Petersfield. The Mid-Hants line did not acquire the expected volume of traffic and the proposed link with Petersfield was not built.

Petersfield lies in a dip in the Portsmouth Direct line between the summits of Haslemere and Buriton. The town's station, like the line, dates from 1859 with its gabled buildings, all attributed probably to the architect William Tite or at least his ideas. On 1st September 1864 the town acquired a route eastwards when the Petersfield Railway Company, sponsored by the L&SWR, opened a line towards Midhurst. At the same time the Mid-Sussex & Midhurst Junction Railway, a nominee company of the LB&SCR, was already pushing westwards from Petworth to Petersfield via Midhurst in an effort to link with the Portsmouth Direct line. Because of a prior territorial agreement between the L&SWR and the LB&SCR, the Mid-Sussex & Midhurst Junction Railway was compelled to end its line at Midhurst and the Midhurst to Petersfield line became the responsibility of the Petersfield Railway Company.

The LB&SCR reached Midhurst on 15th October 1866, two years later than the L&SWR. In all it had taken the LB&SCR seven years between authorisation and completion. Constructional problems were blamed and a tunnel at Midhurst, where a man was badly hurt by a fall of earth, had proved difficult. The local press were highly critical over the delays. 'Wonders will never cease,' said the *West Sussex Gazette*, 'the Petworth and Midhurst Railway, alias "Death's Line", was opened on Monday. This project has been so long in hand we began to despair ...'

With Midhurst reached from the east, there was now a continuous rail link from Horsham (with its London connections) to Petersfield although mostly on LB&SCR rails. However, this had its problems since Midhurst now had two railway stations and they were a short distance apart. On 17th December 1866 a rail connection was brought into use but this required crossing Bepton Road by a bridge which was considered too weak for locomotives. As a result the link was used solely for freight purposes with wagons either drawn across by horses or fly-shunted. Passengers requiring through journeys had to walk! It was not until 1925 after 'grouping' that the Southern Railway

Petersfield station not long before closure of the line to Midhurst in February 1955. The bay was built to the north of the busy A272 to reduce traffic delays. (R.K.Blencowe)

strengthened the Bepton Road bridge and closed the L&SWR station by concentrating all the traffic on the LB&SCR station.

The branch to Midhurst left Petersfield station travelling initially northwards. Prior to electrification of the Portsmouth Direct in 1937, trains could use a main-line loop platform. When main-line services improved, Midhurst trains used a simple bay platform on the north side of the level crossing. In this way too, obstruction of road traffic on the busy A272 Winchester Road could be kept to a minimum. The bay platform was very basic, possessing only one seat and three lamps. Passengers collected their tickets from the main station booking office before crossing the road.

There were two intermediate stations between Petersfield and Midhurst. The first (in West Sussex) was known as 'Rogate for Harting' even though the former was about 1¼ miles away and the latter 1¾ miles away. This station had a passing loop and there was a goods yard. The signal box closed in 1932 and a ground frame was used. On the Petersfield side of the station

136

Ex-L&SWR M7 class 0-4-4T no 30048 at Petersfield due to depart at 12.40 pm for Pulborough, August 1952. (R.K.Blencowe)

there was a private siding to a brickworks. After closure of the line, the station building became a plastics factory. The second was Elsted in an isolated situation named after a village also some distance away. The station had no passing loop, no signal box and the entrance to the goods yard was controlled by a ground frame.

During its last years, traffic on the Petersfield-Midhurst branch was light except on market days. Most passenger trains were worked by 0-4-4T locomotives with classes TI and 02 being predominant. In later years Drummond M7s were used, generally with two or three coaches only. Towards the end, push-pulls were used, both for economy and ease of operation at Petersfield's single platform.

The end came on Saturday, 5th February 1955 when all services from Petersfield to Midhurst ceased. On 6th February 1955 a special train was chartered by the Railway Correspondence and Travel Society and members could enjoy travelling from Pulborough to Petersfield in *The Hampshireman*. Two ex-LB&SCR class E5X 0-6-2 tank locomotives (nos 32576 and 32570) hauled a long train of main-line stock being the last passenger working over the route.

By 1959 the track between Petersfield and the L&SWR Midhurst station had been dismantled. Several bridges have been demolished. One of these was the notorious skew-arch bridge at Ramshill, north of Petersfield, on the main London-Portsmouth road where previously double-deck buses could only pass by driving through the centre. One Sunday morning it was blown up.

13
A 'Battle' And More Lost Causes

The 'Battle of Havant'
Havant/East Southsea
Southampton Terminus

Electric and steam trains at Havant station, 1953. Almost a century earlier there had been a 'battle' near Havant between the L&SWR and LB&SCR companies over running powers over a section of track. (Stations UK)

The 'Battle of Havant'

This book has already highlighted many of the struggles between the major railway companies to gain territories. At the

Rowlands Castle station on the Portsmouth Direct line just north of Havant. In earlier years a brickworks existed on the up-side and many of the bricks were carried away by rail. (Stations UK)

end of 1858, a 'battle' took place at Havant that was the culmination of a struggle between the LB&SCR and the L&SWR over routes to reach Portsmouth. Trains of the LB&SCR had reached the port via Chichester in June 1847 but this did not satisfy London travellers who considered a shorter and more direct route should be available. Neither the L&SWR nor the LB&SCR were interested in such a plan since less miles meant fewer fares collected. So the idea was taken up by the Portsmouth Railway Company which received Parliamentary approval to build a line from Farncombe (already reached from Guildford) to Havant in 1853. The intention was that the Portsmouth Railway Company should build a 'contractor's line' with the idea of selling or leasing when completed to any interested party.

An earlier agreement had given the L&SWR running powers

Hilsea Halt on the electrified line between Havant and Fratton opened in November 1941 – for war workers and at peak hours only. (Stations UK)

over LB&SCR track from Havant to Portcreek Junction north of Portsmouth but the LB&SCR now began to make difficulties. The new L&SWR route was 20 miles shorter than its own via Chichester and part of it was to share their metals. Arbitration failed and the L&SWR, now impatient to use its new line already twelve months completed, announced that a goods train would use the Havant-Portcreek Junction section on 28th December 1858, prior to commencement of a regular passenger service four days later.

On the day, the 'goods train' was manned by almost one hundred platelayers and other robust employees of the L&SWR. On arrival at Havant, three hours earlier than announced, it was found the LB&SCR people were quite prepared. The points had been removed and an engine had been left on the crossing during the night. The points were soon relaid and the engine

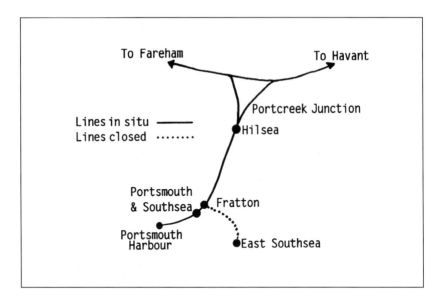

forcibly seized but by this time the 'enemy' had mustered its forces and lifted a rail on the main line, blocking any L&SWR escape. A serious fight appeared imminent but it was averted and, after two hours, the L&SWR men were able to retreat back to Guildford.

The passenger service from Guildford to Portsmouth began as announced but travellers were compelled to travel by bus from Havant. Legal action followed and eventually an injunction was served on the LB&SCR restraining it from interference with through L&SWR running. A fares war followed at considerable loss to both companies before a final agreement was reached. The disputed section became joint property in 1860.

Havant/East Southsea

As a resort, Southsea possessed a singular advantage. Besides becoming popular in itself, it also had a pier. This was used to

A busy Portsmouth and Southsea station, photographed 1967. The Direct Line to Portsmouth was electrified in 1937 when Portsmouth and Fratton stations were enlarged and carriage sheds provided. (Stations UK)

accommodate ferries which plied between Portsmouth and the Isle of Wight.

To the traveller, a journey by rail to reach either Southsea or the ferry service was fraught with difficulty. Before 1885 the train service stopped about one mile short at Portsmouth after which a scramble to attract a cab was necessary. This was made all the more difficult bearing in mind the amount of luggage the contemporary holiday-maker carried. Such difficulties were partly overcome by the provision of a tramway linking the railway and pier, although in the minds of some this was still not completely satisfactory. The result was the Southsea Railway.

The idea was that of one man, Edwin Galt, who, despite being unable to attract sufficient investment initially, succeeded in interesting the two large railway companies in Portsmouth. They were played off against each other and were both soon anxious to subscribe the required finance. How he actually managed to

Fratton station viewed from platform 1, 1967. Prior to 1914 a short branch left Fratton for East Southsea. The branch had lasted only 29 years. (Stations UK)

persuade the L&SWR and the LB&SCR remains a little uncertain today. It has been suggested that some shady dealings might have taken place.

The short 1¼ mile branch from Fratton opened on 1st July 1885. The services were operated by the L&SWR from the outset and it was possible to remain in the same coach all the way from London to Southsea, even if a little shunting was required en route. This latter inconvenience came about because of a junction with the main line at Fratton, the connection facing towards Portsmouth and not, as was really required, towards the capital. There were other disadvantages. One of these was the location of the terminus at Southsea at quite a distance from the pier. Also the Isle of Wight ferry service was now able to operate from alongside a new station at Portsmouth Harbour so further traffic was lost.

Recognising these problems, Galt managed, perhaps surpris-

Portsmouth Harbour, c1930. Before the station opened in 1876, passengers had to cross the harbour to Gosport and then travel by L&SWR branch via Fareham to Bishopstoke (later called Eastleigh). (Stations UK)

ingly, to sell his investment to the L&SWR in June 1886. The L&SWR in turn invited the LB&SCR to take an equal share in the venture. Both were to repent at leisure over such hasty moves. In the meantime the terms of the partnership resulted in the curious situation that each company operated and staffed the line for alternate years. The L&SWR started off the arrangement and continued until 31st December 1886 when all the staff packed up and went elsewhere. The next day the LB&SCR staff took over.

Further problems arose when electric trams came to the area in the early 1900s offering a far more flexible and frequent service. Serious consideration was now being given to the line's future. Early rationalisation took place, only one line being retained for traffic while two new halts were erected at Jessie Road and Albert Road in the hope of attracting extra traffic. In addition steam railcars took over the service.

The steam railcars themselves were curious vehicles which combined an almost conventional steam engine with a coach. The steam engine was very small and was much cheaper to run than a normal locomotive. Unfortunately the engines of these early designs were too small. Seriously under-powered, they were hardly able to move their own weight, let alone a load of fare-paying passengers. After a very short time they were withdrawn for rebuilding, eventually reappearing with larger boilers. Following this the service improved.

Despite such innovations traffic continued to decline, although the losses incurred were modest compared with those of earlier years. The declaration of war in August 1914 was taken as an opportunity to suspend the services and they were never to resume. The suspension was announced at the junction station of Fratton by the following chalked notice:

NO MOOR TRANES TO EAST SOUTHSEA, FISHAL

Southampton Terminus

Southampton's first railway station was opened in 1839 by the London & Southampton Railway (later L&SWR). It was a temporary affair sited near Northam and it was not until a dispute was settled with the Northam Bridge Company that trains could reach the intended Southampton Terminus station. This opened on 11th May 1840 when trains first reached the station, a striking building to the designs of William Tite. Within a short time access was also available to the nearby docks, via a level crossing over nearby Canute Road.

At an early stage it was recognised that the site of the terminus was hardly suitable for an expansion of the network. Although open land was available to both sides, the encroachment of the Solent meant that, if the railway was to extend west or east, new lines had to join the existing route to the north of the station site. Consequently the westward extension to Brockenhurst and Dorchester started from a junction near Northam, while the

Southampton Terminus, c1920. The terminus opened in 1839 and over the years rail traffic increased as Southampton became a major port for transatlantic liners. (R.K.Blencowe)

Southampton to Portsmouth line diverged even further away at Portswood, later St Denys.

Because of this it was necessary to provide an additional Southampton station. Southampton West was built in 1892 on a through line from Portsmouth to Brockenhurst. Yet the original Southampton Terminus had not been forgotten, for a triangular junction allowed trains to run directly from the terminus to Southampton West (renamed Southampton Central in July 1935).

Over the years the port of Southampton developed into the premier passenger port in the country and eventually handled most of the famous transatlantic liners on an almost weekly basis. Much of this expansion was a direct result of investment by the railway company and a former General Manager of the Southern Railway is still commemorated by Herbert Walker Avenue, affording access to one of the many dock gates. The dock facilities developed in two stages, first in the area immediately to the rear of the Terminus station and then on reclaimed land westwards as far as Redbridge. The two were respectively referred to as the Old and New Docks.

Large passenger liners came mainly to the Old Docks, the railway providing a spacious 'Ocean Terminal' for this important and lucrative traffic. Through here the film stars and famous passed, in an age when everyone travelling to the Americas went, out of necessity, by sea. In the New Docks, freight for all parts of the world was the principal commodity and regular mailboats plied between Africa, Australia and India.

Rail communication to both docks was then essential and there was a regular freight service between Southampton and London. The berthing of one of the famous liners would see six or more non-stop special trains run each way between Waterloo and the docks. A connecting railway also ran between the Old and New Docks, but was usually used only for trip shunting due to the sharp curves and numerous unguarded crossings of several roads.

The lines into the docks ran to one side of the Terminus station, while for the ordinary passenger there were, for many years, through London-Southampton Terminus trains. Despite the development of Southampton Central as the principal station for the town, Terminus station continued to be the destination for the many cross-country trains from Reading, Basingstoke, Alton, Didcot and Cheltenham.

The South Western Hotel alongside the station with its massive marbled halls, huge banqueting rooms, vast corridors and bedrooms exemplified the opulent style so typical of Victorian and Edwardian England. It opened in 1872 as the Imperial Hotel but was renamed the South Western at a time when transatlantic liners were transferring from Liverpool to Southampton and became increasingly popular. The hotel is believed to have had its own resident ghost, a 'white lady', who is thought to have been a maid murdered in one of the guests' bedrooms. Another dark story concerns 'coffin-shaped' blocks used in the foundations to commemorate a number of workers who died while the hotel was being built.

The decline in the fortunes of Southampton Terminus came

Southampton Terminus, February 1968, no longer a flourishing rail terminal. As travel by sea gave way to air travel, the importance of the terminal fell away. Passenger traffic ended in 1966. (R.K.Blencowe)

about for two reasons. First, the general reduction in branch line patronage resulted in fewer passengers and eventually less trains as the various services were withdrawn. Second, a world-wide decline in ocean-going passenger traffic in favour of the air routes meant that the ocean liner trade at the old docks evaporated almost overnight. Local interest was transferred to the new docks where in due course a flourishing container terminal was established. By the late 1950s the Terminus station was a sorry sight and looking very run down.

The final blow came in 1966 when, in the run up to electrification of the main line, passenger trains no longer ran to the Southampton Terminus. Although the line is still used for goods traffic much of the station has vanished. The canopies have gone and the platforms have been filled in to make, of all things, a car park. Southampton Terminus building has survived, today Grade II listed and known as Terminus House. After renovation it reopened as Jeeves nightclub on 12th March 1987. It is currently occupied by Stanley's Casino.

Conclusion

The decline of many Hampshire lines began soon after the turn of the last century. Trams and buses were providing a more flexible service than the trains and road haulage was on the increase. The 1¼ mile branch from Fratton to East Southsea was an early casualty closing in August 1914, never to reopen. The following year the short spur to Stokes Bay closed. Moves to develop a ferry link with the Isle of Wight had been stifled by divisions between the main railway companies. The LB&SCR was opposed to any scheme that might reduce its Portsmouth revenue.

More closures followed in the early 1930s. These included the Hurstbourne to Fullerton line and the Basingstoke to Alton line. Originally built as routes to block the GWR encroachment towards Southampton, it was not surprising they should fail as their 'political' needs fell away. Also in 1931, the short branch from Fort Brockhurst to Lee-on-the-Solent closed with the Gosport trams having taken much of the traffic in the Gosport-Fareham area.

The Bishop's Waltham branch closed in January 1933 to passengers. Had proposed extensions linking the town with Ropley on the Mid-Hants line and Droxford on the Meon Valley line materialised then its future may well have been different. Last to close in the 1930s was the line from Ringwood to Christchurch which had been built to provide a route through to Bournemouth. When a route to the resort was opened in 1888 from Brockenhurst, via Sway, the line's future was already in doubt.

In 1935 plans to electrify the London to Portsmouth line were announced but there were doubts about its success. Services began in July 1937 via Haslemere and Havant and the doubts were confounded. The volume of traffic increased and, by 1947, over 7 million passengers were carried annually compared with 3 million in the last year of steam.

In 1948 the railway's finances, effectively wrecked by the Second World War, were saved by nationalisation. With Government subsidies involved it was inevitable that 'rationalisation' processes would follow. Management of the main-line railways was delegated by the British Transport Commission to the Railway Executive with the Southern Region taking charge of all lines in the south. But progress to commence capital investment programmes was slow due to material shortages. In addition integration with other forms of transport, a declared aim of nationalisation, made little headway.

In 1953 there were changes. A Transport Act aimed at decentralisation dissolved the Railway Executive and from January 1955 the Southern Region was controlled by a Board, responsible to the Commission, but with considerable freedom to determine its own actions. Three Divisions were created, the 'South Eastern', 'South Western' and 'Central'.

Despite optimistic plans for redevelopment, freight traffic was still on the decline and the railways were becoming more dependent on passenger traffic. By the early 1960s, the Government's attitude had hardened. In a further Transport Act of 1962, it was clear that commercial viability was considered a more important factor than providing a service to the public. In 1963 the Transport Commission was dissolved and a new Railways Board created. At the same time, the Minister of Transport appointed the Stedeford Group to look at the future of the railways. The findings were not published but one of its members was Dr Richard Beeching (later Lord Beeching), a name that was to become very well known in the years to come.

In March 1963 proposals were made in a report which became popularly known as the 'Beeching Plan'. Basically the idea was to keep lines considered essential to rail traffic and give up the remainder. It had been calculated that one third of the rail system in Britain carried only 1% of the total traffic! The report was considered disappointing in ignoring the potential of many Southern lines, particularly related to electrification. Also by planning the closure of many freight depots, it was thought the report failed to foresee the future of container traffic in the region. Line singling, 'bus stop' type stations for economy and the use of diesel-electric locomotives were other aspects considered overlooked at the time.

As a result of the 'Beeching Axe', many lines closed during the 1960s, leaving the network much as it is known today. Last to go was the Winchester to Alton section which happily today has been preserved in part as the Mid-Hants Railway.

Yet what of the future for Hampshire? Rail privatisation, we were told, would give us an exciting future. Press reports have told us that 'complaints about late, cancelled and overcrowded trains have soared since the start of rail privatisation. Figures point to an alarming deterioration in services.' The Channel Tunnel, although providing rapid links with European capitals, still has to provide high-speed trains in the UK and the tunnel has to prove itself financially.

On a more hopeful note proposals are being considered to provide Light Rail Transit (LRT) systems in Hampshire. The county has a total population of 800,000 who make 1.2 million journeys daily, 80% of these by car. To cope with a looming crisis, it is estimated that £300 million would be needed to upgrade the county's motorways and roads to an adequate standard. Discussions have already been held to provide an LRT system on a Fareham-Gosport-Portsmouth route together with another on the Portsmouth-Waterlooville-Horndean route. A further Fareham-Southampton proposal would involve LRT replacing stopping trains on the Netley railway line, requiring discussions with Railtrack over line sharing. It is argued that LRT in Hampshire would prove considerably less costly than any alternative and necessary road improvement schemes.

As the latest electric trains speed their way through Hampshire from London to Bournemouth, they pass en route some 150 miles of lifeless trackbed, some of which could perhaps have usefully served the community today. Surely many of those early railway pioneers would turn in their graves at the thought of our present depleted railway system and the sad ending of so many fine branch lines.

Opening and Final Closure Dates of Lines to Regular Passenger Traffic

Line	Opened	Final Closure
Southampton Terminus	1840	1966
Fareham to Gosport	1841	1953
Brockenhurst/West Moors/Broadstone	1847	1964
Ringwood to Christchurch	1862	1935
Botley/Bishop's Waltham	1863	1933
Stokes Bay branch	1863	1915
Petersfield to Midhurst	1864	1955
Andover to Romsey	1865	1964
Winchester to Alton	1865	1973
Salisbury to West Moors	1866	1964
Havant to Hayling Island	1867	1963
Southsea branch	1885	1914
Winchester to Newbury	1885	1960
Hurstbourne to Fullerton	1885	1931
Lee-on-the-Solent branch	1894	1930
Basingstoke to Alton	1901	1932
Alton to Fareham (Meon Valley line)	1903	1955
Bentley to Liss (Longmoor Military Railway)	1905/1910	1969
Totton to Fawley	1925	1966

Details of temporary closures before final cessation are given within the text.

Bibliography

In compiling *Lost Railways of Hampshire* the following sources have been used for reference and can be recommended for further reading:

Cooper, Peter *Mid-Hants Guide* (Mid-Hants Railway)

Course, Dr E. *The Railways of Southern England: Independent and Light Railways* (B.T. Batsford Ltd)

Gammell, C. J. *Southern Branch Lines* (GRQ Publications)

Kaurau, Parsons and Robertson *The Didcot, Newbury & Southampton Railway* (Wild Swan Publications)

Oppitz, L. G. *Surrey Railways Remembered* (Countryside Books)

Robertson, K. *The Southsea Railway* (Kingfisher)

Robertson, K. *The Railways of Gosport* (Kingfisher)

Turner, K. *Pier Railways* (Oakwood Press)

Williams, R. A. *The London & South Western Railway Vols I and 2* (David and Charles)

White, H. P. *A Regional History of the Railways of Great Britain Vol 2: Southern England* (David and Charles)

INDEX